Thank...
I hope that you enjoy...
that it inspires you to visit Africa
someday (if you haven't already
been here)

Peace,
James
'02

12 DAYS IN GHANA

REVELATIONS, REUNIONS
AND REFLECTIONS

By

James W. Gaines, Jr.

ISBN: 1-4033-2519-7 (e-book)
ISBN: 1-4033-2520-0 (Paperback)

This book is printed on acid free paper.

1stBooks - rev. 09/18/02

Table of Contents

Introduction vii
Map of Ghana ix
Friday, June 16, 2000 1
    Brooklyn Bound 1
Saturday, June 17, 2000 4
    D-Day (Departure Day) 4
    Go-Go To Get Going 4
    Ghana Airways 5
Sunday, June 18, 2000 7
    We Finally Arrive 7
    Gotta Watch Your Back 7
    Body Vapors 8
    Arrival at Hibiscus Guest House 8
    Off to the Cape – One Africa 9
    The People of One Africa 12
    The Juneteenth Celebration 13
    A Star is Born (Yeah, right!) 14
Monday, June 19, 2000 16
    KaKum National Park 16
    You can take a Man out of the Ghetto… 18
    The Outdoor Shower 18
    The Peace Corp in Africa 19
    Mable's Table 19
Tuesday, June 20, 2000 21
    Wassa Domama 21
    Journey to the Sacred Rock 21
    Back in the Village 22
    Attention to Detail 22
    Preparing for the Dungeons 23
    On the Catwalk 27
    The Last Supper 28
Wednesday, June 21, 2000 30
    Sunrise on the Cape 30
    Denzel Washington 30
    Good-Bye Cape Coast 30
    The Road to Kumasi 32
    Public Restrooms 32
    Better Late than Never 33

The Cozy Lodge..33
Sir Max 34
Dinner and Desserts 35
Thursday, June 22, 2000 ....**36**
Beware of the Chicken Curry 36
The Grass Choppers 36
Persistence Pays Off 36
The Asantehene..37
Graceful Walkers 38
Well, He did Offer… 39
Traffic 39
Yao's Relatives 40
Is it Really Denzel? 40
Village of the Kente Weavers 41
On the Way to Accra 42
Return to Hibiscus 43
Friday, June 23, 2000 ....**44**
Chillin' Out..44
Mrs. Hayford..44
Late Night Snack 45
Saturday, June 24, 2000 ....**47**
Out of Sick Bay...47
The Big Mystery 48
The Name Game 48
Arrival at the Palace...49
The W.E.B. DuBois Center......................................50
Dr. Maulana 51
Labadi Beach 52
Lucy 54
Sunday, June 25, 2000 ....**56**
Meeting The Obodi Chief.......................................56
Service at the Guest House 58
Anxiety Sets In...58
Dansomah 58
The Boateng Clan 60
Papa..61
The Family History 61
Back at the Guest House 63
NaNa Kow 63
Learning about the Armstrongs 64
More on NaNa Kow..64
Party Over Here 64

Dancing Queen..66
August, My Man 68
Big Sista Wakeelah 68
Pure Silliness..69
Monday, June 26, 2000..**71**
Dog Tired 71
The Road to Odumase..72
7-11 76
The Numerologist 76
Tuesday, June 27, 2000 ....**78**
Surprise, Surprise..78
Keeping Our Fingers Crossed 81
The Nkrumah Memorial..81
The Cultural Center..84
A Family Affair...85
Mystery Solved 87
Wednesday, June 28, 2000 ....**88**
The Final Days...88
A New Identity 89
Winding Down...89
"Special Sauce"...90
Our Final Evening at Hibiscus..91
'Til Next Time 91
Thursday, June 29, 2000 ....**93**
The Middle Passage 93
Touchdown 93
Grumpy Old Man...94
Ghana in D.C. 95
The Future..95

Introduction

The following is the travel log from a journey to my mother's homeland, Ghana, West Africa. The journal describes a personal quest to learn more about my maternal roots and to make a physical connection with my ancestral homeland. As a "returning son", it also chronicles the daily interactions with my travel companions as well as the emotional highs and lows surrounding my discoveries.

This is not meant to be an all-encompassing view of the entire country of Ghana, as most of my journey was spent in and around the southern Ghanaian cities of Accra, Cape Coast and Kumasi. It is my sincerest hope that my travels will inspire others to make a trip back to their homeland to obtain a feeling of wholeness that comes with knowing who you are.

Map of Ghana

Map courtesy of www.theodora.com/maps, used with permission.

Friday, June 16, 2000

Brooklyn Bound

I was happy to say that the day started off somewhat uneventful. With the exception of the previous night's sleeping arrangements, I had hoped that the first leg of our journey to Ghana would have a similar conclusion. Instead of meeting my sister and spending a relaxed evening at her house as originally planned, I ended up staying at my house for the evening. With so many errands to run and phone calls to return, I was running late. And of course, I hadn't finished packing.

I ended up getting to bed around 12:30 AM. I wasn't worried about being tired for the trip though, since I knew I didn't have to drive to Brooklyn. My sister Lavelle (aka Sandra Gaines) and I had decided to catch a bus to New York a day before our flight to Ghana from JFK International Airport on Saturday. It wasn't glamorous, but we knew the bus provided an inexpensive and relatively hassle-free means to our destination. Leaving early also gave us extra time in case anything unforeseen happened. We were determined not to miss this flight.

Rising before the sun at 4:20 AM, I got dressed and loaded up my car that my friends affectionately referred to as "the limo", a 1991 Oldsmobile with almost 200,000 miles on it. Several days earlier, I made arrangements to leave my car at my uncle's house so he could keep an eye on it while I was away. I reached his house by 5:20 AM, and my sister arrived shortly thereafter. We then made the short ride to her friend Rocha's (pronounced "Ro-shay") house in Northeast D.C. so that she could drop us off at the Greyhound bus station.

Rocha had a top of the line BMW, so it was nice to arrive at the bus station in style. People still knew that you're fronting though, how fly can you be if you had to take the bus? Soon we were pulling our luggage through a terminal that seemed crowded for an early Friday morning. We ended up waiting in line for our bus, and while doing so, struck up a conversation with a young Howard University student going to New York to visit relatives. I teased Lavelle, saying she should make her romantic overtures to him on the bus trip. Lavelle made a comment about not mixing business with pleasure since she worked at Howard, and we left it at that.

We caught the 7:00 AM bus to New York. We've all heard nightmares about riding Greyhounds. From being trapped sitting next to someone with bad hygiene, to being seated next to a nasty bathroom, it was hard to know

1

what to expect. Lavelle's friend Jay thought we had lost our minds because we were taking the bus. He told her he wouldn't be caught dead on one of those things.

Surprisingly, the bus ride was a pleasant experience, despite our reservations. The ride was relatively quiet, with the exception of occasional outbursts from a young child. Along the way, I read a very interesting article by a writer who had recently visited Ghana. This article, along with my previous readings, really heightened my excitement about our journey.

We arrived at Port Authority in New York at about 11:00 AM. We waited at the terminal so we could meet the co-owner of one of the properties in Ghana where we would be lodging. While waiting, I was approached by a scruffy looking brother trying to sell me a gold bracelet wrapped in a used napkin. I was like damn, brother could have at least found a clean napkin to display the goods, not that a clean napkin would have moved me to buy the bracelet anyway. After I brushed him off, the "salesman" moved on to another potential customer.

We waited some more and finally, Lavelle saw the coordinator, Imakhus. She and her husband were originally from New York and had since relocated to Ghana. She had briefly returned to the States for treatment of an unspecified medical condition.

Imakhus was a very pleasant woman who seemed very grounded. She greeted us with warm hugs that made her seem like a familiar relative. She wanted us to carry over a bag of sports videos for her husband to watch along with a father's day card. I appreciated the fact that she didn't wrap the videos so we could see what it was she wanted us to carry. The last thing Lavelle and I needed was to be duped into carrying contraband for some unscrupulous individual.

We chatted for a bit and gave her another hug before we jumped into a cab headed for my friend Mike's place in Brooklyn. Mike was one of my best friends from high school and I'd always enjoyed talking to or hooking up with him. I considered he and my good friend Carlos to be the brothers I never had.

After fighting our way through the thick New York traffic, we finally arrived at Mike's place at Flatbush and Bergen in Park Slope Brooklyn. We dropped off our bags and got Mike caught up on our plans. Of course, we laughed and joked as we always did, right before he had to go to work. After Mike left, my sister and I went to lunch and later that evening, took in the new Shaft movie, starring Samuel L. Jackson. The movie was so-so, not bad, but not great either. I gave it two stars (out of four).

On the walk back to Mike's apartment, I noticed a full moon in the sky. I wondered if we would see the moon the next night in Africa. I thought that it would be nice to stroll a beach in Accra while I contemplated my future (marital issues, job issues), hoping for some insight with the moon as my companion.

Saturday, June 17, 2000

D-Day (Departure Day)

Lavelle was the first to wake up, and she had already showered by the time Mike and I got up. We all got ready and walked to a small restaurant downstairs for breakfast. While we ate, we discussed various topics, including our trip, the challenges of life, love and relationships.

Lavelle also talked about a loud street argument she overheard during the night. There's something about the phrases "bitch" and "where's my money?" that were sure to get things going on a hot Friday night in any town, let alone New York. We had a good laugh because I had warned her of that before we arrived at Mike's apartment, speaking from experience since I'd visited him before. You know what they say about this city, it never sleeps. It seemed like the night just wouldn't be complete without your typical loud, drunken cursefest.

Go-Go To Get Going

We finished up our food and walked over to a local hardware store, where Lavelle picked up a few last minute items. We went back to Mike's place to finish packing and make sure we had everything for the trip. While we got ready, Mike started an impromptu jam session when he cued up an oldy but goody on his CD player. After a few seconds, the familiar opening notes of Rare Essence's "Body Moves" came thundering out of his speakers. He turned it up louder, and in moments, we were all grooving. Mike and I went over a few high school dance steps as we laughed and joked. I asked Lavelle to take pictures to capture the moment.

Mike Summey and James Gaines, Brooklyn, New York

After a couple of songs and breaking a sweat, we reluctantly turned off the go-go and loaded up Mike's truck with our luggage. On the way to the airport, Mike popped in his Trouble Funk tape. It was cranking! Here we were, on the way to JFK bopping our heads to the sounds of D.C. The music was a great send-off and placed us all in great spirits!

Ghana Airways

Mike dropped us off at Ghana Airways at JFK around 1:00 PM. Our flight didn't leave until 4:00 PM, but we wanted to allow ourselves plenty of time to check in and relax before our flight. There would be no O.J. commercials in the airport that day, at least not from us.

We made our way to the check-in counter, where we ran into the third member of our traveling group, Monique Armstrong. She was a student at Morgan State University taking advantage of a great opportunity to see

Africa. When most kids her age were worried about which nightclub they're going to, she was out there taking on the world. She'll definitely go far.

We all checked in our luggage and met her family upstairs. We had met them all before at a "get-to-know-you" dinner before our trip. We talked as we took the long walk to our terminal. I got to know Monique's father (Roy) a little better. He was cool. Her mother (Marie) and brother (Royce) were cool as well.

Eventually, we bade her folks farewell and walked through security to the pre-boarding area. From the looks of things, you could see it was going to be a crowded flight to Accra. We sat with the other passengers in the pre-boarding area. We were surprised to see the same people who checked our bags were the same people now getting ready to announce the boarding arrangements. Ghana Airways must have hustled to get those folks all the way across the airport. They really needed to hire some more people.

What was even more surprising was when everyone suddenly jumped from their seats and bum-rushed the door when no announcement was made! We quickly jumped in line too, thinking maybe they were giving away something free. There was no order to the boarding whatsoever, just a mad scramble. Through the chaos, we eventually boarded the plane for our 9 1/2 hour flight to Ghana.

Sunday, June 18, 2000

We Finally Arrive

We finally arrived in Accra's Kotoka International Airport at 7:00 AM local time! Lavelle and I were tired, but very excited. Monique suffered through a brief bout of airsickness, but she soon recovered.

Once we got off the plane, things continued to seem disorganized. We passed through a doorway framed with a colorful sign that read "Akwaaba", or welcome. We went to the area where the airport officials stamped your passport. Wakeelah, the trip organizer and our group leader, had already been in Accra for several days and was to meet us at the airport when we arrived. We didn't see her, but we figured she must be in another part of the airport waiting.

Gotta Watch Your Back

In the meantime, a Ghanaian police officer saw the three of us and acted as if he was going to look after us by helping to get our luggage. I got bad vibes from him when he asked to hold on to our passports. Not knowing what was up, I reluctantly agreed, making sure to keep my eyes on him. As we waited for our luggage to come around on the carousel, Wakeelah came up behind us. Lavelle and Monique hugged and greeted her while I elbowed for position at the luggage belt.

Lavelle told Wakeelah about the police officer having our passports, and she instinctively knew that he was up to no good. She walked over and politely asked the officer for the passports. Knowing he wasn't supposed to have them, he smiled and gave them to Wakeelah. She then good-naturedly asked him to keep an eye out for us. That's Wakeelah, the Great Communicator, smoothly diffusing a potentially difficult situation. She was a communications professor at Morgan State University and her expertise served us well in this moment.

After I retrieved our luggage, we made our way to the truck. As we approached the truck, several airport baggage boys surrounded us. They tried to chat us up and get cozy by using played-out American slang like "what's up homey!". When the truck pulled up, they swarmed our bags and tried to put them in the truck for us. We were yelling "No, no! We've got it!" Of course, we were ignored. And thus began our first glimpse of how hard it was for many folks to make it in Ghana. Some said that due to government corruption, Ghana's resources had been squandered. A few politicians got rich, while the vast majority remained poor. The bag boys were so aggressive because they desperately wanted that tip.

As I walked to the passenger side of the truck to get in, the bag boys asked for a tip. Pretending I couldn't really understand what they were saying, I mumbled something and got into the truck. Wakeelah told the kids that we didn't ask for them to put the bags in the truck and they ignored us when we asked them to stop, so no tip. They were pissed, and we drove off.

Body Vapors

One of the things you noticed in Ghana and many other places outside of America was that not everyone used deodorant. This was not to say Americans had a monopoly on good hygiene because we had our share of people with this problem. All I can say was you definitely noticed it more in Ghana than the U.S. Some families saw this as a luxury. If you're poor and you only had enough money for either a ham sandwich or a can of Right Guard, you'd choose the ham sandwich every time. So in a way, I could understand the situation. Some people believed that a strong smell was a sign of virility, while others just didn't know any better, plain and simple. None of this made it any easier to breath, but I understood.

After getting in the truck with Yao, our driver, this was one of the first things you noticed. He was a small man, about 5'- 6", maybe 140 lbs. He didn't say much when we first got in the truck. He seemed like a nice guy, but being in a confined space with him was olfactory punishment. As we drove, he would occasionally put his arms up to stretch. Everyone in the back would gasp. I was in the front seat, so I just turned my head. But I really felt for my sisters in the back seat because there was no escape.

Arrival at Hibiscus Guest House

Yao drove us to our first destination, the Hibiscus Guest House in Accra. It was in a middle class neighborhood that felt sort of like a typical American suburb. There we met the establishment's owner, Ama. She was a tall, beautiful dark-skinned woman with a soft voice.

We dropped off our luggage, showered and got ready for breakfast. Theresa, a worker at Hibiscus, brought us our food. The food was OK except for my oatmeal, which was soupy. I hate soupy oatmeal. Anyway, they tried. I ended up eating fruit, toast and fresh squeezed orange juice.

Monique Armstrong, Sandra Gaines, Wakeelah Mutazammil, Hibiscus Guest House, Accra, Ghana

After breakfast, we all took out enough clothes to last a couple of days and packed them into smaller travel bags. There was a Juneteenth[*] celebration in Cape Coast that we wanted to attend, so we decided to leave then instead of several days later as we had originally planned.

Off to the Cape – One Africa

We loaded the truck and got on the road for our drive to Cape Coast. Once we reached the outskirts of Accra, we noticed how rugged the roads were. We definitely needed a 4-wheel drive vehicle to pass through some of the towns. On the way, we saw miles and miles of poor villages broken up by plush greenery and ads for Guinness beer. When I asked our driver about the beer ads, he let out a sly laugh. He didn't say anything else, but I knew he knew all about that Guinness beer.

---

[*] Juneteenth is one of the oldest known African-American celebrations. It celebrates the ending of slavery in the United States. Union generals arrived in Galveston, Texas on June 19, 1865 to announce that slavery was over. This was a full 2 years after President Lincoln's Emancipation Proclamation had become official on January 1, 1863.

Surprisingly, it wasn't as hot as I thought it would be. We'd come during the rainy season, and at that moment it was overcast with temperatures in the 80's.

After about two hours on the road, we arrived at One Africa in Cape Coast. One Africa was owned and operated by Imakhus and her husband NaNa Okofo. Imakhus was the woman we met in the Port Authority who asked us to deliver the packages to her husband. Before we reached the property, we passed through what looked like a poor, dilapidated neighborhood. But when the guard opened the gates to One Africa and we drove in, I was pleasantly surprised.

We saw a beautiful lawn framed by six small, circular chalets. Each chalet was named after famous African-Americans such as Malcolm X and Harriet Tubman. The main house anchored the property. The land sloped down towards the beach and the mighty Atlantic Ocean (Gulf of Guinea). It was an awesome sight to see. As I viewed the horizon, I saw the Elmina slave dungeon in the distance off to the right, and I couldn't help but think about our ancestors dying out there in that water.

As we walked across the lawn, NaNa Okofo, the man of the house, greeted us. NaNa was one of the many African-Americans who had relocated to Africa. He described himself as. an "African-Ascendant", ascending to a higher order, a higher state of mind. He and his wife were Hasidic Jews and very knowledgeable about African history. They were very committed to investing their time and energy into rebuilding Ghana.

Sandra Gaines, George Culmer (standing), NaNa Okofo, James Gaines, Wakeelah Mutazammil at breakfast, One Africa, Cape Coast, Ghana

We eventually reached our rooms. Each of us had our own chalet. We all couldn't get over how beautiful everything was, not in a ritzy kind of way, but in a "one with nature" kind of way. We unpacked and got ready for lunch.

Kwaku, our chef, had prepared an excellent meal and had set the outdoor table so we could eat with the soothing ocean at our side. The food was fantastic! He fixed a very healthy dish of rice with fish and a small salad. This was the first of many superb meals from Kwaku. During the meal, NaNa Okofo came out and hugged each of us. He then sat down with us for a more relaxed conversation.

After our meal, we went for a walk on the road in front of One Africa. The road was not paved and very rough. As we walked, several young boys eventually started following us. They welcomed us to Ghana, and then immediately asked for our addresses. When we declined, they offered us their addresses. They were looking for an American to "sponsor" them, i.e., send them money.

Through our brief conversation with the youths, we learned that the Ghanaian school system was quite different from ours. Families had to pay to send their children to school after elementary school. Junior high and senior high school were not cheap. Many families couldn't afford to send their children to school, so some children resorted to these tactics. I couldn't say that I wouldn't do the same if I were in their shoes. I understood their plight, and I told them that I would send money through One Africa.

The People of One Africa

While there, we met many wonderful people who frequently dropped by One Africa. We learned that one Africa was one of the places where relocated African-Americans would pass through. Some of these people included the following:

- **BaBa VanKirksey** – An African historian and former engineer from the States.
- **George Culmer** – An older gentleman from Philadelphia, very well read. He liked to have fun, and he could drink a little bit too.
- **Gladys "Auntie" Rice** – A retired nurse from Detroit. She worked as a nurse in Cape Coast villages. She had lots of energy and was a great storyteller.
- **Jafare/Wife/Son Bongo** – A very free spirited family. Jafare went to grad school at University of Maryland while his wife described herself as a "citizen of the world". She was pregnant with their second child. Bongo, their son, was a precocious kid who was into everything. Everyone adored him.
- **Cohane/Mable/Kwame/young daughter** – One Africa neighbors that owned the bar/restaurant called Mable's Table next door. Cohane was African-American and Mable was Ghanaian. Cohane was another well-read, activist-type brother involved in local issues affecting Africans.
- **Joey** – He was one of NaNa's friends. We were told he owned several businesses in Ghana. He also had a penchant for smoking some strong ganja (marijuana).
- **Winnifred** – A Ghanaian who worked at One Africa as a domestic. She had a beautiful smile!
- **Brother from Mississippi** – This gentleman lived across the road. He had moved to Ghana within the past year.
- **El Shabazz** – A younger brother from Brooklyn about my age, also a Hasidic Jew. He was full of energy and also very knowledgeable about history.
- **Kwaku** – He was another gentleman (not our cook, but another Kwaku) from the U.S., Baltimore to be exact. He was a thin

older guy with gray hair and glasses. He was also very knowledgeable and was very funny.

- **William Jones** – A graphic arts teacher at one of the colleges in Ghana. He was about our age and also hailed from Brooklyn.
- **Jeneba** – A very peaceful, spiritual, soft-spoken young woman, about our age. She had just been in an auto accident and had a sore neck. She also worked at One Africa.
- **Marlon Hite** – A young brother from Southern University. He worked in the Peace Corp and had a two-year assignment in one of the villages not too far from Cape Coast.

While we were in Cape Coast, we also learned about some of the customs and sayings that were native to Ghana or imported from America. Among them were the following:

- **"Bruny" or "Obruni"**– A white person or foreigner. Also, a derisive term used to describe African-Americans perceived as being snobbish.
- **Taking a Joe Louis** - Taking a quick wash-up where you don't hit anything below the belt. This was more of a New York term that NaNa once used.
- **Dashing** – A small monetary hook-up you gave to someone who had done something nice for you. This could also mean giving someone a bribe.
- **Chop** – To eat or get something to eat.
- **I'm coming** – This was said when you were leaving, meaning you were going out and coming back later. This took a while to get used to hearing.
- **Meet me** – Phrase said to someone when you were trying to offer something of yours such as food. Equivalent to saying "Would you like some?"
- **Cedi** – Ghanaian unit of money. During our visit, 5000 cedis were worth roughly $1.00.
- Never call a Ghanaian "crazy" or ask **"Are you crazy?"** This was the greatest insult you could say. I didn't know the origin of this and I was very curious to find out how this came to be.

The Juneteenth Celebration

After the long trip, the fantastic meal and meeting all these people, I was dragging. I tried to stay up so my body clock would start to adjust. I was having a difficult time trying to stay awake after dinner. There was a

13

Juneteenth dance later that evening and I seriously considered skipping it all together. I went to my room and slept for a about an hour.

I woke up feeling temporarily rejuvenated. Nighttime had settled in on the Cape, and everyone was about to leave for the evening's festivities. We gathered at the vehicles, where the faint smell of ganja permeated the air. We got into the truck and after about a 20-minute drive ended up at a small plaza in the city. There was a band set up outdoors, with chairs surrounding a grassy area and dozens of people waiting to get in. We each paid about $1.00 as an entrance fee.

NaNa went to the microphone and said a few words regarding Juneteenth and the purpose of the celebration. Afterwards, a few members of the band assembled in the grassy area where we were sitting. The drum players and bongo players started a strong beat. Out of the darkness, a dance troop slowly materialized on the grassy dance floor.

The group feverishly went through their routines. First the men performed, then the women, then together as one cohesive unit. Each group danced with so much energy that it seemed like the grass would catch fire. A slight rain briefly fell, but it soon passed. After the dance troop performed, the crowd was warmed up.

The rest of the band took to the stage and began to perform. This was the crowds' cue to get up and dance. The children searching for sponsors were there as well. They again hit us with their requests for addresses. I again explained that we would send money through One Africa. After a few songs, we sat down and let others dance.

A Star is Born (Yeah, right!)

At one point, NaNa went back onstage to play with the band. He picked up a small, hand-held percussion instrument and joined the beat. El Shabazz, one of the young brothers from Brooklyn, was singing. The band started to play a few familiar Bob Marley tunes. They sounded as if they were ad-libbing, just going with the flow. Feeling energized from my nap and for some reason a little bold, I decided I would go onstage to see if they would let me sing. I tried to get Lavelle to go with me, but she chickened out. I approached NaNa and asked if I could sing with the group. He enthusiastically replied "Sure!" El Shabazz gave me a mike, put his arm around me and said, "Let's show them how we do it in the States!"

We launched into "No Woman, No Cry", or at least the parts that we knew, each of us alternating between lead and background singing. I even threw in a few Chuck Brown lyrics, telling the crowd, "I want to see people, not signs." My sister and Monique couldn't believe what they were seeing.

This was a little out of character for me, and no, I hadn't been drinking. Needless to say, I had a blast.

After singing, I talked to some of the members of the dance troupe. They told me how hard they practiced and how they too were looking for sponsors. As good as they were, they needed to be dancing at the Kennedy Center or something. I left wishing I could do more to help them.

After a little more dancing, we finally piled in the truck and went back to One Africa. When we arrived, I retired to my chalet for a deep sleep.

Monday, June 19, 2000

KaKum National Park

It was early morning and Kwaku awakened us by walking through the grassy One Africa courtyard ringing the breakfast bell. I had slept well. Kwaku made our breakfasts to order. I had oatmeal, toast, fruit and tea. His oatmeal was the bomb! Everyone agreed as we wolfed down our meals.

This morning, we were going to a rain forest in KaKum National Park. We finished our breakfasts, got dressed and drove to the forest. The visitors' area at the Park had a touristy feel to it. It had a Rain Forest Café, although not the ones that we had in America, and a gift shop. Wakeelah paid our admission fees, and we waited for our guide.

We sat down on a bench that had small chameleons scampering about. I decided to go to the restroom to make sure I was on "empty" before we went into the woods. I didn't want anything biting me in the ass while I took care of business!

Eventually, we were assigned a guide. He gathered us around and introduced himself before leading us into the forest. Before we could get far, the guide asked if anyone had a knife. When we said no, he said it's OK and beckoned for us to follow him. Being city folks, we all instinctively stopped and looked at each other. Lavelle and Wakeelah asked our guide why we needed a knife. Were we going to have to stab something out there?

The guide reassured us that we would be OK and that he only needed the knife to cut leaves and bark to show us while we walked through the forest. We all laughed, breathed a sigh of relief and followed him through the woods.

The guide told us many interesting facts about the plants and leaves found in the rain forest. He showed us plants used for furniture, houses and sources of water. He also showed us a live African bee's nest, and told us that there were bears and other dangerous animals in the woods.

Park Guide showing us the unusual plant life in Kakum Rain Forest, Ghana

At one point, our guide stopped and looked off into the distance through the woods. I asked him what he was looking at and he mentioned that there was a Sacred Shrine in the woods not too far from where we were. We wouldn't be able to see it on our hike, but he mentioned it was definitely worth checking out if we ever got the chance. We continued our hike until we got to the canopy walkways.

These walkways were suspended hundreds of feet above the forest floor. They were very narrow and didn't appear to be very sturdy. Each person had to go across one at a time. The guide went first, then me, then Wakeelah. We quickly learned that Wakeelah was scared to death of heights! Halfway through and gripped with terror, she was seriously questioning her own decision to walk across the rickety footbridges. The guide had to come back to escort a frightened Wakeelah across. We all eventually made it and we applauded Wakeelah for conquering her fear.

We worked our way back through the rain forest to where we started. Our driver wasn't there and had gone down the road to "chop" or eat. We waited a few minutes until he returned. The total hike was about two hours, and we were ready to "chop" ourselves.

Before we left, we presented our guide with a small gift for successfully leading us through the rain forest and helping Wakeelah get through the canopy walkways. We knew he was just doing his job, but in Ghana, it was customary to give small gifts or money ("dashing") to people who had done excellent job or to someone who looked after you.

You can take a Man out of the Ghetto...

We returned to One Africa where we got ready for lunch. Kwaku hooked us up with another culinary masterpiece at the outdoor table. While we were eating, George, another American transplant from Philadelphia, got into an argument with some guy who was staying in one of the chalets. He was dressed like a pimp and George had taken offense to how this brother was treating the woman he was staying with.

We all wondered what was about to jump off, thinking damn, we couldn't get away from this type of activity even on vacation. We were all especially concerned for young Bongo, since George was holding Bongo's hand while he was yelling. He eventually stopped arguing and came down to our table to join us for lunch. While we were eating, we told George about our rain forest adventures.

The Outdoor Shower

After lunch, I decided to use the outdoor shower which was located in the center of the property but closer to the ocean. It had a small cylindrical stone wall about chest-high with one showerhead. It was definitely an adventure. While showering, I was staring directly into the power of the ocean that was only 50 yards away and it left me wondering about the secrets it contained. Again, my eyes noticed the Elmina slave dungeon and traced a path across the open water searching for the trails left by slave ships as they carried off my ancestors.

I wondered how many of our brothers and sisters were at the bottom of that sea, choosing death over the inhumane circumstances. Part of me was hoping that the ocean would whisper something to me, let my ancestor's voices come alive in the ocean's roaring winds. My mind continued to ponder these questions until I noticed the darkening skies.

You don't realize how vulnerable you are until you're standing naked looking at an ocean whipped into a frenzy by storm clouds. The darkening skies snapped me out of my pensive mood as my thoughts turned to finding shelter. I quickly finished my shower and returned to my chalet. I got dressed and left my screen door open to catch more of that ocean breeze.

After about 20 minutes, the clouds cleared up and I stretched out across my bed to do some reading. I read about half a page before I was knocked out. There's nothing like a little jet lag and ocean breeze to put you to sleep.

The Peace Corp in Africa

I woke up feeling well rested. We lounged around a bit and eventually got together for dinner. After dinner, Marlon stopped by. We found out that he was a student from Southern University in Louisiana and was in Africa as a Peace Corp volunteer. He was stationed at a small village not too far from One Africa. During this conversation, we arranged an impromptu visit to Marlon's village for the next morning.

He also mentioned a Sacred Stone that was not too far from his village. It turned out that this was the same Sacred Stone that the KaKum guide had mentioned earlier. This was our chance to see this structure as well as visit Wassa Domama, Marlon's village. We agreed that we would meet at 7:00 AM the next morning for our trip.

Mable's Table

Later that evening, we went next door to visit with Cohane and his wife, Mable. George decided to join us. Before we sat down, we talked to an American student sitting at another table. She was at the Juneteenth function the night before, and she complimented me on my singing. It was nice to see that my brief stint as a singer earned me at least one fan from the crowd.

We eventually sat down at another table and began to talk to Mable. Cohane was not home but he was to return shortly. We met their young son, Kwame and her young daughter. George was having fun and was trying to get Lavelle drunk. Lavelle sampled some alcoholic concoction, but she knew her limits. George ordered some food for everyone to enjoy. I passed since I was still full from dinner. Cohane had finally arrived home and joined us for some good conversation.

We discussed African politics, both national and local. We started to talk about how local leaders were involved in an effort to beautify the slave dungeons, almost to the point of turning them into some sort of twisted theme park.

They reportedly had repainted the dungeons, scrubbed the floors, and even installed a gift shop and eatery. A gift shop? An eatery? Can you believe that?!? Who in their right mind would want to have lunch in a slave dungeon? You know Jewish people wouldn't stand for this sort of thing, so why should we? Cohane was one of the main agitators that led to the stoppage of this process. We all agreed that the "Disneyfying" of the dungeons had to cease.

We eventually walked back to One Africa after our long and interesting discussions. George looked to be a little tipsy, and Wakeelah supported him as we left. It was hard enough to walk on those roads while sober. We all eventually headed back to One Africa, where we retired for the night.

Tuesday, June 20, 2000

Wassa Domama

We got up at around 6:00 AM so we could eat breakfast, meet Marlon and go to his village. Breakfast was again superb. Before we knew it, Marlon had arrived and it was 7:00 AM. George decided to join us on our trip to Marlon's village.

We piled into the truck and left One Africa for Wassa Domama. Yao seemed to have a good grasp of Ghana's roads. The one thing that struck everyone was that "not far from here" to Marlon was very different from our definition. Marlon's village was FAR. It took a good 45 minutes to get there! And the roads were treacherous. D.C. potholes had nothing on these unpaved roads. You could consider this to be off, off, off road driving! We finally arrived at Marlon's village, where we met some of the people as they went about their daily activities. They were very nice people. The village was poor, but tidy. Even their outhouse had no smell. I mean it smelled downright clean.

Journey to the Sacred Rock

We met a few more people and then picked up two guides to ride with us out to the Sacred Rock. We got back into the truck for more off road driving. After another 30 minutes, we reached roads where even the truck couldn't go. It was now time to hike. Everyone figured we'd hike for about 10 minutes, and then see the structure. Guess again.

We ended up hiking through the rain forest, up hills, down hills and through mud for another 45 minutes, all the while sweating like crazy and wondering what the hell were we doing so far out in the bush. We finally arrived at an outdoor room framed by huge upright rocks that formed the walls of the shrine. These rocks supported another large slab that formed the roof. We sat for a moment to catch our breath and take it all in before the guides proceeded to tell us the story of the rock.

They mentioned that villagers used to worship at the formation where libations were poured. The structure could shelter up to 200 people. The guides also mentioned that the black stains on the walls were believed to make people fertile if they were ground up and used as an enema.

The shrine was no longer used, but you could see the remnants from previous inhabitants. We took pictures, walked around the structure, and then started the long trek back to the truck. Along the way, George was drenched with sweat and Wakeelah's knee was bothering her. We had to stop several times for folks to catch their breath. One of the stops was at a makeshift rest area that the villagers built out of thatch and small pieces of wood. We snacked on some fruit that one of the guides picked along the way.

We eventually forged ahead. On the way back, we ran into a villager who had some "rot-gut" liquor called Apateche that George wanted to purchase. We bought the liquor and took pictures of some of the villagers. We finally made it back to the truck, tired, sweaty and funky.

As we drove along, we bounced up and down along the unpaved roads until we reached Marlon's village. We oozed out of his truck and hung out in his crib for a minute. It was small, but cozy. His house had a living room/study and a bedroom.

Marlon's main mode of transportation was his mountain bike. .If something happened to someone out there and some simple first aid couldn't fix it, as we say in the city, you're just ass-out. There were no phones, no internet, no TV's, no electricity, no 911. It would take a monumental effort to get some help back there.

Back in the Village

While we rested, Marlon and our guides prepared some fresh cut pineapples for our refreshment. Man, did that hit the spot! After we recuperated, we presented our guides with small gifts for leading us through the rain forest. They were very appreciative. We took some more photos and talked to some villagers before we got into the truck for the ride back to One Africa.

On the way back, we passed a schoolteacher walking along the dirt road, just getting off from work. We offered her a ride to her home area. She accepted our offer and jumped in the back with me. I'm thinking, OK, she probably lives around the corner or something, we can save her a few steps. If you could have seen where we picked her up and where we dropped her off, she probably had another hour of walking ahead of her. And we complained about our commutes to work! People in this village walked like this everyday, like it ain't no thang. This was absolutely amazing.

Attention to Detail

We finally got back to One Africa, just a mass of odor and fatigue. Lunch was ready, so we all took quick wash ups and sat down to eat. As usual, Kwaku's food hit the spot. After expending all that energy, this was just what we needed. After lunch, I took another outdoor shower. This time, the weather was perfect, sunny and warm.

After relaxing again in my bungalow, I went to the laundry house to pick up my clothes. My laundry was neatly ironed and folded. They even ironed my draws! And my clothes were CLEAN. Somebody did some serious scrubbing.

Preparing for the Dungeons

I went back to my room to get myself ready for our visit to the Cape Coast slave dungeon. Having heard of how the dungeons affected returning Americans, I didn't know what to expect of myself. Would I cry? Would I break down? These questions left me feeling a bit uneasy.

Eventually, we loaded up the truck and drove towards the dungeon. As we approached, I noticed how the dungeon dominated the block it sat on. This white-washed building sat in the middle of town almost majestically. I could see why so many people mistakenly referred to it as a "castle". If you didn't know it's shameful past, you could easily be fooled by its outward appearance. Hell, you'd halfway expect some lovesick princess to reside inside. But those who knew the building's dark history knew this wasn't a prop in anyone's fairy tale.

I guess that's why people wanted to mask the pain that emanated from those walls by turning it into a remodeling project. Thank God for people like Cohane who fought against those efforts. What those folks needed to realize was that you shouldn't be made to feel comfortable in this place. You should be disturbed when you passed through those walls, because what happened there was real. To have it any other way would be a grave injustice to our ancestors who suffered at the hands of their oppressors.

When we reached the entryway, we were told by one of the workers that they were about to close for the day. Because NaNa was well known in Cape Coast, they decided to give us a break and let us go through anyway. We were escorted past two huge wooden statues that honored our ancestors. Each statue had chains and the unknown faces of our ancestors emerging from the hell of slavery.

We went through to the main courtyard of the dungeon that opened up towards the ocean. The perimeter of the courtyard was lined with cannons that seemed to be ready for firing at a moments notice. As I walked through I thought about the madness that went on there hundreds of years ago. I wondered if any of my direct ancestors were ever trapped inside the bowels of this building.

Main Courtyard, Cape Coast Slave Dungeon, Cape Coast, Ghana

Pretty soon, a 21-year-old guide named Amissane Hackman joined us. He took us on a tour of the upstairs section of the dungeon, where the English, Dutch and Swedes once held court. They had sections for church officials as well as sections where slaves were branded and sold.

**Amissane Hackman, guide explaining the history of Cape Coast Slave
Dungeon, Cape Coast, Ghana**

Amissane also talked about the layout of the dungeons and showed us
where the soldiers stayed. As we returned to the courtyard where we started,
Amissane wanted us to know that contrary to what we'd been told, many
Africans did not view African-Americans as Bruny's.

He said that he welcomed us and looked at us as brothers and sisters. He
also told us how emotional he was about slavery and how the whole thing
still touched him very deeply. He was so moved by this that he couldn't take
us on the tour of the holding cells. He left that task to NaNa. At this point,
we said good-bye to our young brother, and NaNa took the lead.

NaNa gave each of us candles, and lit them just before we entered the
dungeons. Standing at the threshold of the dungeon, the first thing that hit
me was that this was not a place where any human should be. It was dark,
intimidating, daunting, hot, sad. With each step down the labyrinth-like
passageway, I felt my insides tighten as the walls seemed to constrict around
us. I had the eerie sense of my own freedom being stripped away. And this
was with me knowing my stay would be brief. It was at this point that I
really felt for my ancestors.

Yao, Wakeelah and James at the entrance to the Male Slave Dungeon, Cape Coast, Ghana

There were only five of us in the dungeon, and we were sweating. Could you imagine 500 of us crammed in there at one time, no light, nowhere to lie down, no toilet? You went to the restroom right there on the floor. I could not imagine the pain, the fear, the utter desperation that they went through. The floor that we were standing on was actually years and years of compacted waste and skin cells from our ancestors. This was deeply disturbing.

As we walked through with our candles lighting the way, we were encouraged to call out names of ancestors who had passed on. I started off by calling out my grandfather's name, Nesbie Gaines, who had passed away the year before. Soon everyone did the same. In a strange way, you really felt as though you were connecting with their spirits.

Yao was deeply moved by everything. Strangely enough, that was his first time visiting the dungeons. Monique had tears streaming down her face and Lavelle was so moved that she couldn't speak. As we walked along the dark paths that our ancestors took, we reached the infamous "Door of No Return". This was the last door our ancestors walked through before they were crammed into a boat bound for the Americas.

The curators here had done a wonderful reversal of this. The outside of the door was labeled "Door of Return". We triumphantly marched back through the doors, symbolically allowing our ancestors to return to their homeland through their children. As we came back through the door, we sang a joyful song celebrating our ancestors' return.

After we went through this ceremony and ended up on the outside of the dungeon, we were again swarmed by the same children who hit us up before. This particular dungeon sat in a fishing village, so it was not uncommon to see children playing in and around the dungeon. The children also knew that this was a prime area for American tourists and that many were emotionally vulnerable after the dungeon experience.

As we exited the dungeon, the children addressed us by name and again asked for our addresses. Once again, we politely told them that we would contact them via One Africa. We all realized that this was something we had to get use to while in Ghana.

Another tragedy in all this was that according to Amissane, many Ghanaians were not fully aware of what really went on in the dungeons. Amissane explained this to us and mentioned that he had taken it upon himself to learn more about slavery after witnessing visitors break down in tears as a youngster. He went to the library and it was there that he learned about it. But the average Ghanaian was not taught this in their normal school curriculum. He told us that for the most part, slavery was glossed over like some insignificant blip on the radar screen. Slavery's legacy has unfortunately left people on both sides of the Atlantic with a fractured knowledge of our history. Hopefully, more and more Ghanaians and African-Americans will strive to seek the truth about our past so that we can enlighten others. We must establish a reconnection!

On the Catwalk

After the dungeons, we desperately needed something to lift our spirits. We drove a few blocks and ended up stopping at Nana-Ata Fashions run by Lucy, a local seamstress. She created incredible fabrics and outfits. Monique wanted to buy some fabric for her mother and I had no intentions of buying anything. So why did I end up buying a three-piece abada?

27

James in his abada

After trying it on, everyone told me I looked sharp! Yao, Lavelle, Wakeelah, Monique, Lucy, even Lucy's mother whole-heartedly approved the selection. And the price was so cheap when compared to American standards, I had to buy it. I was short on cash so Wakeelah paid and I settled with her when we got back to One Africa. Before we left, Lucy assured me that she'd contact me and use me as a model for her fashion catalog. We were joking, of course.

The Last Supper

After everyone made their purchases, we drove back to One Africa. This was our "last supper" with Kwaku at One Africa, since we were leaving for Kumasi in the morning. Kwaku hooked us up with a vegetarian dinner consisting of a dandelion salad, yams, and plantains. The meal was tremendous as usual. Afterwards, we gathered in NaNa's house to discuss our feelings about our visit to the dungeon. We were all advised to take showers to wash away our ancestors spirits before we went to bed. I complied and turned in for another good night's sleep.

Wednesday, June 21, 2000

Sunrise on the Cape

Lavelle had arisen early and was already dressed by the time I got up. Since this was our last morning, we decided we would get up early enough to greet the sun as it peeked over the horizon. Myself, Lavelle and Monique went down on the rocks by the ocean so we could get an unobstructed view of the sun in the eastern sky.

We hoped that the clouds would clear up and let the sun shine, but they did not cooperate. By the time we saw sunlight reflecting off of the clouds, we realized it was too late. Oh well, that gave us something to do the next time we visited.

We moved from the rocks to the breakfast table. This was our last meal at One Africa before we continued our travel agenda. Many of our new friends stopped by and chatted with us while we ate. NaNa, George, Brother Shabazz and Jeneba were all there to see us off.

Denzel Washington

Since we were on our way to Kumasi for a meeting with a University Vice Chancellor, we were all dressed up for breakfast. While we were eating, NaNa commented that I looked like Denzel Washington. I laughed, but he was serious. A few minutes after he said this, Brother Shabazz walked up and sat with us. NaNa asked Brother Shabazz whom did he think I looked like, without revealing his own opinion. Brother Shabazz, who hadn't heard NaNa's earlier statement, said the same thing: Denzel Washington. This time everyone laughed. The ladies teased me about this for several days thereafter.

Good-Bye Cape Coast

As I mentioned before, it was customary to present small gifts or "dash" someone who had taken good care of you. We all decided that the small gifts we had were not enough to give to NaNa. We agreed that we would send him a package in the mail after we returned to the States.

We then had to decide on what to do for Kwaku, our most excellent cook. During our stay, we found out that Kwaku was doing all of this hard work while suffering from diabetes. His eyesight was failing him and he needed glasses, but he couldn't afford to purchase them. So our gift to him was to give him enough money to order a pair of glasses. We collected about $50 and presented him with the money. He was thrilled. Kwaku was very thankful and he even joked with us about sending us meals via e-mail. Ha! We wished!

After we presented Kwaku with his gift, I ended up talking with Brother Shabazz, my reggae-singing partner. Somehow he and I got to talking about our marital situations. He told me how hurt he was that his wife and young son, whom he delivered, were back in the U.S. I told him about me being separated from my wife and how I felt. We ended up saying how important for us as black men to support each other in times like this and how our situations weren't so uncommon. There were a lot of folks out there going through similar issues. We dapped each other up, hugged and vowed to keep in touch.

We moved over towards the rest of the group so we could take one last "family" photo at One Africa. After the photos, we packed up the truck, said our last good-byes and headed towards Kumasi for our meeting with the Vice Chancellor of the University of Science and Technology (UST).

(Standing) George Culmer, James Gaines, NaNa, Jeneba, Monique Armstrong, Kwaku (Kneeling) Brother Shabazz, Sandra Gaines, Yao, One Africa, Cape Coast, Ghana

31

The Road to Kumasi

We left Cape Coast and drove north towards Kumasi. Since we had been up so early, it didn't take long for us all to fall asleep during the car trip. I woke up a short while later and wondered why we were going so slowly. We were behind about 20 large construction trucks on the way to a building site. Since the road could only hold two-way traffic, it took some time before Yao was able to get in front of the construction convoy. This put a serious dent in our travel time. We knew there was a good chance we would be late for our meeting with the Vice Chancellor and we definitely didn't assume he would understand "CP-time".

To take my mind off of our impending tardiness, I asked Yao to teach me some Ga words so I could surprise my mother. Years earlier my mother had explained to me that we were from the Ga tribe located in the eastern region of Ghana. Yao recited a few words and I dutifully jotted them down, thinking of how I would spring them on my mom when I returned home.

Along the way, we saw many miles of poor villages and tropical greenery covering acres of flatlands. This pattern was occasionally broken up by a gas station or mini-mart. In some towns, we saw goats crossing the road or just walking along the side.

Public Restrooms

Men and women relieving themselves on the side of the road in broad daylight was a common sight in Ghana. It's funny because before we left, my mother had warned us about the high probability that we would have to resort to such methods. We prepared ourselves by always carrying around a roll of toilet paper and a package of handy wipes. It was our version of American Express; in other words, don't leave home without it!

On the way to Kumasi, it was finally time for me to "pay my water bill". I instructed Yao to pull over as soon as he saw an inconspicuous patch of road. Praying that no one walked up on me or drove by, I did my thing, hit the wipes and we rolled. Lavelle had to go too, but she held on and told Yao to stop at the first service station.

About 30 minutes later, we reached an Elf gas station where the ladies used the facilities. After a brief rest, we continued on our journey towards Kumasi.

Better Late than Never

We arrived about two hours late for our meeting with the Vice Chancellor. When we pulled up, we ran into him in the parking lot where he was speaking to students. He came off as a very gracious person who commanded respect. After introducing ourselves, he invited us up to his office where his staff scurried around, answering his every request.

Vice Chancellor Anyi politely mentioned that he couldn't sit long with us because he had other meetings to attend. Since we were late, we couldn't say much. He sat long enough for us to ask him a few questions and present him with a bowl from Morgan State University. We handled him well, coming off like U.S. Ambassadors.

He agreed to pose for a few pictures before he handed us off to his second and third in command. They sat longer with us and answered more of our questions about the university. The Vice Chancellor had mentioned that they were responsible for showing us the university and some of the sights in Kumasi.

One of them, Mr. Danzo, agreed to help us coordinate our agenda. Along with seeing the University, one of our main objectives while in Kumasi was to meet the Asantehene, viewed by many as the most powerful chief in Ghana. Ghanaians generally agreed that the Asantehene had more power than President Rawlings himself. We agreed to meet the next day for a brief tour of the University before we traveled to the Asante palace.

The Cozy Lodge

After coordinating our plans with Mr. Danzo, we left the university and drove a few miles to our hotel, the Cozy Lodge. Wakeelah went in to let the hotel people know we had arrived, while the rest of us remained in the truck. We eventually got out of the truck and moved to the outdoor patio/dining area where it was much cooler. After about 15 minutes, Wakeelah came out and told us that the hotel had given away our rooms. See what happens when you're late? Eddie, the hotel manager who sort of looked like Faison Love from the TV show The Parenthood, walked towards us with Wakeelah.

He told us that he didn't want us to be stranded, so he made arrangements for us at another hotel a few miles away. As long as we had a place to lay our heads, we knew we would be fine. Feeling relaxed, we decided to stay for lunch.

We ordered our food and chowed down once it was served. After we finished, we all used the facilities and got cleaned up from our meal. Wakeelah wiped her hands with a handy wipe which she mistakenly said contained "spermicide". She said this twice before I asked her what type of handy wipes was she using. We all laughed when she finally realized what she was saying.

We said a few words to the manager and waited for our check. We noticed that our server had gone to the back and had disappeared for a long time. The manager had started to walk towards the main building, away from the dining area. We all got that look in our eyes and started to ease our way to the truck, knowing we hadn't paid.

We calmly got into the truck and began to pull off, thinking we had just gotten over. When we saw the manager walk back towards the dining area and say a few words in African to our server, we knew we were busted. The manager flagged us down and politely mentioned that we didn't pay the bill. Wakeelah, the Communications Professor, put all of her skills on display when she artfully said, "Oh, I thought you were treating us since we were inconvenienced with the rooms." A less experienced person would have told the driver to hit the gas pedal and dared the manager to stop us. Wakeelah paid the man and was able to get him to offer us a free meal the next time we stopped by his establishment. Now why'd he have to go and say that?

Sir Max

After a short drive, we arrived at the Sir Max Hotel. It was a decent place with a pool and restaurant. The rooms had cable TV, radio and AC. That was all I needed. We hadn't watched TV since we left the States, so this was a nice change of pace.

We got settled and met in the lobby to plan our agenda for the evening. We decided to give Yao the night off so he could party with his friends in Kumasi. Yao had friends all over Ghana and seemed to know about every hangout in the country. We knew Yao was ready to get loose and party a little since he had been hemmed up with us for all these days. We decided to just stay in for the evening and catch up on our journals and post cards.

I decided to take advantage of the hotel pool, since I hadn't exercised since I had been in Africa, with the exception of hiking through the rain forest. Lavelle decided to sit out by the pool and write in her journal while I swam. Monique and Wakeelah stayed in their rooms.

I swam for about 20 minutes, doing the breaststroke for several lengths of the pool. After an insect stung Lavelle, we made a hasty retreat inside. We ended up in my room where Lavelle continued to write in her journal. I took a shower, shaved and took a brief nap while Lavelle wrote.

Dinner and Desserts

After about a 30-minute nap, I got up to meet everyone for dinner. It was about 8:00 PM and it was raining very hard. Even though we were in the rainy season for Ghana, this was the first real downpour we had encountered. We gathered in Monique's room, where Yao was waiting with a duffle bag. He had brought some kente fabric from one of his relatives and wanted to see if we were interested in purchasing. It was a large piece of fabric for which he wanted $100. Wakeelah and Monique passed.

Yao headed out to party and we went to the restaurant for dinner. I ended up eating the curry chicken with rice, while everyone else ate desserts. Lavelle sampled a little of my chicken curry, and then finished her dessert. The food tasted good and we left the table satisfied.

We went back to Monique's room where we joked around, made plans and relaxed. In the middle of our conversation, Monique got up and went to the bathroom. We continued to joke around, and Monique returned with a serious look on her face. She was concerned that the braids in her hair were pulling her real hair out. Wakeelah reassured her that everything was all right. We ended the night by confirming our plans before we retired for the evening.

Thursday, June 22, 2000

Beware of the Chicken Curry

We got up at 6:00 AM for our return visit to the University. I initially felt OK, but after showering and going downstairs for breakfast, I started to feel queasy. I felt tired, almost like I had the flu. Immediately, my mind started racing. Did I have malaria? Was it something in the pool from last night's swim? Was it the chicken curry? I was just hoping it didn't get worse.

I was able to eat a good breakfast before we left for the day. As we were packing the truck to head to UST, we ran into some local youths trying to sell us their wares. Apparently, someone had tipped them off that Americans were staying in the hotel. Their appearance was more than pure coincidence, since they were waiting on the road near the back parking lot where our truck was parked.

We walked out to where they were and surveyed their goods. Everything they showed us was either too bulky or too expensive. We asked them to show us some more stuff, and they agreed to go and get some more. They ended up taking a long time to get the items, so we eventually left.

The Grass Choppers

On the way to the UST campus and throughout Ghana, we noticed young men in the fields cutting grass with machetes. Cutting grass like this was backbreaking. What would normally take minutes with a push mower took hours with a machete. I wondered why they didn't at least purchase a non-motorized push mower. Some people couldn't afford this type of mower, and it seemed that others used this grass cutting method as a form of punishment. You would occasionally see solitary school children chopping grass in the field while their classmates played. And let's just say they weren't smiling while they were working.

Persistence Pays Off

After a short ride to the UST campus, we pulled up to park. Before we could get out of the truck, a taxi pulled up and screeched to a halt beside us. It was the boys with the goods that we had asked to see. Once they realized we had left, they jumped in a cab and tracked us down. Since we were early for our appointment, we decided to look at their items.

They had some nice leather and straw bags. The lead talker was named Kweise. He looked sort of like a swollen, broke Sisqo from the R & B group Dru Hill, platinum hair and all. We negotiated and haggled, but eventually we all made purchases.

The Asantehene

After wrapping up our business dealings, we met up with Danzo for our tour of the campus. Danzo seemed like students and fellow administrators were pulling him in 400 different directions. He asked us to wait a few minutes while he finished up a few tasks. When it became apparent that he would be longer than he originally planned, we decided that we would skip the campus tour and head to the Asantehene Palace and Museum, where we hoped to get a meeting with the Asante Chief. Danzo, looking relieved by our decision, agreed to meet us there later.

On the way to the museum, I felt worse. I felt really tired and wondered if I was going to get sick. I rolled the window down and just kept quiet in an effort to conserve energy. We finally reached the museum. We noticed everyone was dressed in black or red, traditional funeral colors in Ghana. We learned that the Asantehene's brother had died, and that he would be unavailable to meet with us. A meeting with the Asantehene would have been a huge deal, and we were disappointed that we would not have the opportunity to meet with him.

We decided to go ahead with the tour of the museum. A tour guide met us and walked us through the main courtyard of the palace. As we made our way to the museum, we passed beautiful peacocks with brilliant feathers. The tour guide took us through the museum, where we learned about the history of the Asantehene. We saw pictures and wax figures of past Asantehenes, and he told us the story behind each. While he was talking, I was trying to keep my head from spinning.

We ended up in the gift shop where we purchased some trinkets. I had to use the restroom before I left, because I was not trying to do what I had to do on the side of anybody's road.

As we were leaving the gift shop, Danzo was outside waiting for us. He proceeded to try to get an audience with the Private Secretary to the Asantehene, who was sort of like a vice president. We found out that he too had a death in the family and was out of town for the funeral.

Danzo was able to secure a meeting with the Acting Private Secretary (APS) to the Asantehene or the third person in the chain of command. After a short sit in the waiting room, we were ushered into the office with the

APS. We took a seat on the couch, and Danzo sat in a chair facing us. The APS sat in a chair with his back to us facing Danzo. It was protocol for the Asantehenes and their officials to not speak directly to their guests, but to a middleman. The middleman then repeated everything the chief said. Even though they spoke perfect English, this was the custom.

Wakeelah told Danzo that we'd come to ask for the Asantehene's blessing to assist him in raising money for his scholarship fund by getting help from historically black colleges and universities (HBCUs) in the States. Danzo relayed the message to the APS. The APS politely asked us to put the proposal in writing so that the Asantehene could study it further when he had time.

At one point, the APS broke custom and looked directly at me. He asked me if I'd ever worn the traditional robe that they were wearing for the funeral. I didn't quite know what to say. I was caught off guard, not knowing if I should speak or what. I said something, and he joked about how difficult they are to wear. We all laughed before we got up to leave.

As we were leaving, one of the guards offered us some peacock feathers and asked us to 'dash' him. It seemed like everyone had a side hustle, even the palace guards. Wakeelah obliged and we finally walked back to the truck.

Graceful Walkers

I still felt queasy, but I was encouraged because I wasn't getting worse. When we got to the truck, we quickly grew frustrated because Yao was nowhere to be found. While we were waiting for Yao to show up, I took a picture with a woman balancing what seemed like a million peanuts on her head in several bowls. Throughout our trip, I'd seen people balancing everything from logs to fruit, to dishes, to laundry. You name it, our people could balance it on their heads with a baby strapped to their backs.

I had seen men and women walk up hills and over rough terrain while balancing enormous piles of stuff on their heads and not once did I see someone drop something! Hell, I dropped stuff using my hands, let alone balancing something on my head! All I knew was that if my family depended on me to transport food like that, we'd starve, because I would have spilled most of it in the street.

Wakeelah, Mobile Merchant selling peanuts, James clowning

Well, He did Offer...

Yao finally showed up, and we decided to go for lunch. At this point, I had no appetite and I decided not to push my luck by eating. We decided to go back to the Cozy Lounge to get our free lunch from Eddie.

Everyone ate except for me. I had hot water with lemon. I took this along with some Imodium AD to help "dry me up", so to speak. Eddie tried to be slick and offered to pay for half of the lunch. Wakeelah, again using her well-trained communication mind, told him, "Don't play me, Eddie". Needless to say, Eddie kept his word and paid for our lunch.

After we ate, one of Eddie's friends came over and told us about "Queen Latifah" performing in Ghana. We were like *the* Queen Latifah? He replied no, just someone using her name. I guess the real Queen would never know.

Traffic

Shortly after driving away, we saw a truck turned over on its side with a broken front axle. People stared and traffic was brought to a crawl. Traffic in Ghana was definitely different than the States. You rarely saw posted speed limits, and once you got outside the major cities, you could forget about traffic signs and traffic signals. While driving in the city, people routinely ran red lights. I was surprised we hadn't seen more traffic accidents.

Yao's Relatives

After we ate, we went to Yao's aunt's house. The roads were again about as rugged as they came. We bounced along the unpaved roadway until we reached the house. We walked through a wide, muddy yard with chickens scurrying around the main house. The house was surrounded by a fence and was large by Ghanaian standards.

Yao's cousins and his aunt greeted us. The inside was very nice, with plush furniture. His relatives were very warm people and they treated us like long lost relatives. You immediately felt the love. Wakeelah jokingly told Yao's aunt that she wanted her to adopt us. His aunt told us that the next time we came to Kumasi, we must stay with them.

Is it Really Denzel?

While we were talking with the family, I noticed Yao's female cousins staring at me and giggling. They appeared to be about my age. You could tell they liked what they saw. We got to the point where we were ready to take pictures, and they giggled even harder when I stood next to them for the photo. I decided to mess with them by putting my arm around them for the picture. Yao seemed to get mad and asked me to switch places with him for the next picture, moving me away from the one who was doing the most giggling. I wasn't concerned, and we took another picture.

After the pictures, we moved outside. The girls were giggling more and wanting to hug me. At one point, Wakeelah told the girls that I was Denzel Washington. They really giggled and ran inside the house! Even though they didn't understand English very well, they knew who the hell "Denzel Washington" was! Wakeelah told them that "Denzel" was traveling with them trying to check out Ghana on the DL.

The one with the pretty smile came back out, grabbed my hand and told me something in her native language. I asked Yao to translate what she said. She repeated what she said for him to hear. He looked at me with a strange face, and said she complimented my shirt. Bullshit! By the way she was holding my hand and gesturing, I knew she wasn't just complimenting my shirt.

We took some more pictures, and exchanged addresses. Yao's aunt cried as we left, saying how sad she was going to be since we were leaving. Keep in mind we had just met her. I say this not to belittle her feelings, because I believed they were genuine. It just goes to show you how loving the Ghanaian people were. Even though the country didn't have the material trappings of America, you couldn't beat the care and hospitality they showed towards their fellow man.

Village of the Kente Weavers

I still felt bad, but I knew that if I could just lie down, I'd be straight. Well, before we could get on the road for our three-hour drive south to Accra, we had one more stop.

Monique wanted to buy some kente fabric, so we decided to stop by Bonwire, the kente weaver's village. After another 30-minute ride, we arrived at the village. The village was run down and looked raggedy. The people looked desperate. I was surprised, since this place was known all over Ghana as being one of the major manufacturers of genuine kente cloth.

As our truck pulled up, kids trying to sell every type of kente you could imagine immediately surrounded us. You would have thought we were the Jackson 5 or something. Since I already wasn't feeling well, having a whole bunch of kids tugging on me and shoving addresses in my face was downright annoying. Despite this, I managed to maintain my composure. We finally made our way through another muddy courtyard to the shop where the cloth was produced. Again, the kids were like locusts! Strangely enough, I never felt like I was in danger, it just took some getting used to having all those people around you like that.

Since I knew I wasn't buying, I took on the role of security for our group, asking the youths to step back and give the ladies some breathing room. The sheer desperation of the kids was depressing. It's really disappointing when you realized that there's only so much you could do and that you couldn't help everyone. At every village we visited, the kids approached us in the same manner, looking for that elusive sponsor. This just made me appreciate how lucky I was in that I didn't have to go through this when I was growing up. In comparison, we were very fortunate.

Kente weaver, Bonwire, Ghana

After the ladies made their purchases, we made our way back to the truck. Again, kids clung to us, we could barely get into our vehicle. Eventually, we were able to drive off.

Before we got on the road for our drive to Accra, Yao stopped at a chophouse to get something to eat. This place was as rundown as they came and definitely wouldn't pass a Health Department inspection. Despite this fact, Yao was not deterred. He ordered his food and wolfed it down while we sat in the truck. After he ate, he was good to go for the night.

On the Way to Accra

With Yaos appetite satiated, we finally departed for Accra. It was dusk, and we really wanted to avoid driving long distances at night. Some of the roads were really bad and the lighting nonexistent. There was no AAA to save you if something went wrong. If you had a problem, you were SOL. So we didn't feel comfortable leaving at that hour, but we figured we'd make the best of it.

I was still feeling lousy, so I again resorted to conserving my energy by sleeping and staying quiet. Along the way, we saw many shopkeepers on the side of the roads closing up for the day.

About half way through the trip, Lavelle and I had to get out to use the "restroom" on the side of the road again. How elegant.

Monique, who was usually quiet and reserved, really began to open up. During the drive, she discussed her past relationships, while Lavelle and Wakeelah offered their advice. I definitely stayed out of that conversation! I was not trying to step on any landmines.

As we approached Accra, we listened to a radio talk show. The show consisted mostly of the announcer repeatedly saying "Hello?" while some happy, Caribbean-type music played in the background. It was incredibly banal and the last thing we needed to hear after an exhausting road trip.

Return to Hibiscus

Three hours later, we arrived at the Hibiscus Guest House, tired and cranky. Hibiscus was the first place we stopped when we arrived in Ghana. Yao had done an excellent job of getting us there safely.

We unloaded our gear and found our rooms. I took a shower and went out to the lobby where Wakeelah and Ama, the owner of the guesthouse, were talking. I placed my order for a light dinner and went back to my room to chill until it was ready. A few minutes after lying down, I was off in dreamland. I was awakened by a phone call telling me that dinner was ready. I staggered out of bed and went down for dinner.

The food looked good, but I had no appetite. Also, it was late, so I couldn't eat a lot anyway. I wanted to go straight to bed when I finished, and I didn't want to be kept awake by indigestion.

So I ended up nibbling a little, chatting a little, then finally going to bed. I laid down hoping that I'd feel better in the morning.

Friday, June 23, 2000

Chillin' Out

I woke up feeling achy, but I felt a little better than I did the day before. At least it wasn't malaria. I decided to get up and wash my face. Wakeelah stopped by my room to check on me. Since we had been on a non-stop, whirlwind tour, Wakeelah advised me as well as everyone else to rest while she ran errands.

Before she left, Wakeelah decided to have breakfast. Lavelle and I went with her while Monique slept in. I had a light breakfast, and I was glad that my appetite had returned. During breakfast, we talked about the poverty that we'd seen in Ghana. Wakeelah told us that Ghana was one of the better countries in Africa when it came to poverty. I was a little surprised when she said that, since we'd seen a lot of poor villages.

After breakfast, I went back to my room to rest while Lavelle, Monique and Wakeelah went out. I ended up spending most of the day resting and writing in my journal. After sleeping and writing for several hours, I stepped out on my balcony for some fresh air. The lawn at Hibiscus was beautiful. When I leaned over my balcony, I saw Yao on the balcony next to mine, just cooling. We greeted each other and shook hands. He asked me how I was feeling and jokingly asked when I was coming back so that he wouldn't be trapped with the ladies. I assured him that I was regaining my strength and I told him I would be ready to go in the evening.

Later on, I hooked up with the crew for dinner. At this point, I felt much better and I was ready to eat. No more chicken curry dishes for me! I played it safe and ordered fish and white rice. We continued our conversation about Africa and the conditions of some of its other countries.

Mrs. Hayford

After dinner, Lavelle and I waited for our Uncle Frankie's sister-in-law, Mrs. Josephine Hayford, to meet us at Hibiscus. She arrived at Hibiscus at about 8:00 PM. She was a manager at a bank in downtown Accra. When we greeted her, we immediately felt her bubbly personality. She looked like an older version of her sister Rebecca, whom I'd met the previous year. She had the same cheeks, same eyes and same smile as her sister. She also had a wonderful laugh. We talked and got her caught up on our travel adventures.

Auntie Josephine Hayford

We mentioned that we tried to get a meeting with the Asantehene, and she revealed that she was very close to him. Apparently, he used to be a customer at her bank. Wakeelah commented that we would surely mention her name if we got a chance to meet the Asantehene.

Before she left, we confirmed our plans for the weekend. We agreed that we'd get together on Sunday around 1:00 PM so she could take us to meet my mother's cousins in Dansomah.

Wakeelah and Monique left while Lavelle and I sat a while longer with Mrs. Hayford. After a short period of time, we walked her to her car and went back to our rooms.

Late Night Snack

After we returned to our rooms, we ended up meeting in Wakeelah's room for some ice cream and cookies. I bought along some double chocolate chip cookies as a snack, and we all had a sweet tooth. Even though the ice cream we ordered was freezer burned, we devoured our desserts. A short time after we finished, Wakeelah was conked out. We decided to leave her so she could sleep.

I ended up going to Lavelle's room to chill for minute before going to my room. We both discussed the upcoming meeting with our relatives and wondered what they would be like. I was really looking forward to meeting them and seeing the region from whence we came. Before I left, I reminded Lavelle that the next day was "Lariam* Day"

*Lavelle and I were prescribed Lariam pills to ward off malaria.

Saturday, June 24, 2000

Out of Sick Bay

This day, I woke up feeling much, much better. I woke up early without a phone call. I went to the bathroom to get ready for the day when the phone rang. It was Lavelle, wondering why no one called to wake her up. I mistakenly figured she was already awake, since she usually got up before everyone else.

We eventually walked over to the dining room for breakfast. I ordered an omelet with fruit and toast. The food was pretty good, and we had good conversation as usual. After eating, we jumped in the truck to go to Ba-Ba's house. Ba-Ba was another older brother from the States who knew a lot about Ghanaian history. In addition to being an historian, he was an engineer, an author and a screen playwright. He seemed to be an all-around Renaissance man if there ever was one, although some people would beg to differ. We later learned from Wakeelah that Ba-Ba had burned a few bridges during his stay in Africa and had developed a somewhat shady reputation. On this day, he was going to take us to see a Ga chief from the Obodi tribe.

During our trip, Wakeelah revealed that her husband Wali was able to trace his roots back to the Obodis. He had returned to Africa the previous year and was enstooled* as a chief and given land to develop. Wali was currently in the U.S. completing training for a new job. He eventually planned on returning to his tribe and to his homeland. This visit to the Obodi chief allowed Wakeelah to introduce herself as Wali's wife and for us to pay our respects.

We headed to Ba-Ba's house taking another bumpy road. After a short ride, we reached Ba-Ba's neighborhood, but we couldn't quite find his house. Apparently, there was some confusion about the directions. We ended up at some stranger's house. A young black woman came to the gate. We explained our plight and she let us use the phone. Shortly after that, an older white man came out. We all wondered if she was his woman or his maid. I commented that she was acting a little too casual to be the maid.

Wakeelah eventually got ahold of Ba-Ba, and he gave us the final directions to his place. We picked up Ba-Ba and went towards the Chief's palace. We started to talk to Ba-Ba about our family history and about how we were trying to reconnect with our roots. With his knowledge of Ghanaian history, Ba-Ba was able to help us piece together part of our history. Yao

---

* ritual for making someone a chief

47

also contributed to the discussion. Based on the names that we mentioned and the region of our family's origin, we were able to learn the following from our conversation:

- **"Matey"** - Our grandmother's maiden name, was from the Ga-Krobo tribe, and was considered a royal name. This name was generally from Dodowa, a city in the Eastern region of Ghana.
- **"Sikapa"** – Our grandfather's name had several meanings, including "old gold", "good money" or "good looking". This was generally an Akan or Krobo name.
- **Krobos** and **Akans** were generally from the Eastern Region of Ghana.
- **"Shai"** people generally were from Dodowa

The Big Mystery

Lavelle and I were also trying to piece together the mystery of our grandmother's movements while in Ghana. Our mother had never given us a lot of details regarding where our grandmother lived. We knew that after my grandfather died, she no longer lived in our grandfather's village and ended up living in Dodowa. This gave us the impression that she may have been banished from her village for some reason.

Lavelle and I felt uneasy about letting too many people know our family's past until we knew what had happened. The last thing we wanted was for someone to try and run us out of town because of whom we were related to.

The Name Game

We also discussed traditional Ghanaian names and how they were derived. Many Ghanaians named their children according to the day of the week that they were born and the order in which they were born. We learned that this was generally an Akan tradition, but other tribes in Ghana, including the Ga tribe, had adopted it. The names for the days of the week along with male and female names were as follows:

English Day	Akan Day	Male Name	Female Name
Sunday	Kwasida	Kwasi	Esi
Monday	Dwoda or Djoda	Kwadwo	Adwoa
Tuesday	Benada	Kwabena	Abena or Araba

Wednesday	Wukuda	KwaKu	Ekua or Aku
Thursday	Yaoda	Kow or Yao	Yaa or Aba
Friday	Fida	Kofi	Efua or Efia
Saturday	Miminda	Kwami	Ama

I originally thought I was born on a Tuesday, so people began calling me "Kwabena". However, when I returned home, I found out I was actually born on a Sunday, so I should be called "Kwasi". I was also told that the word "Baku" meant "first born" or "first born son". So my name would be "Kwasi Baku".

Arrival at the Palace

We finally reached the Ga-Obodi chief's neighborhood, but we didn't quite know how to get to his house. We rolled up on a group of young men playing checkers. Ba-Ba asked one of them to show us where the chief's house was located. He jumped in the back with me and directed us. After a few twists and turns, we finally reached the house.

Ba-Ba got out and knocked at the gate. After a few seconds, a woman who turned out to be the chief's wife greeted us. She was a tall, dark-skinned woman with broad features. She told us that the chief was not home, but he might return shortly. She invited us in to wait for him on their veranda. The house was still being built, and it looked like it was going to be something on a grand scale. Before we sat down, Lavelle asked to use the restroom and was soon led away.

As we made our way to the veranda, we walked through a courtyard filled with wild turkeys running loose. Soon after we took our seats, a young servant brought us water. As we drank, Ba-Ba continued to educate us on Ga history. I continuously had to swat away flies that had seemingly come to listen in on our conversation.

After a few minutes, the chief's wife returned and told us she was not sure when her husband would return. She told us that we could meet with him the next morning at around 7:00 AM, right before he left for church.

We agreed to the early appointment and soon after said good-bye. As we left, Lavelle told me about her "traumatic" experience in the restroom. Putrid, acrid, foul, malodorous, any word you can use to describe "straight-up fonky", was how she depicted it. I was just glad I didn't have to use it.

We got to the truck and took the young brother back to his corner after dashing him. From here, we went to the W.E.B. DuBois Center*.

*W.E.B. DuBois was the first African-American to obtain a PhD from Harvard. A tireless Civil Rights worker, he was a key figure in the Harlem Renaissance and helped found the NAACP.

The W.E.B. DuBois Center

We drove for about 20 minutes before we reached the center. We pulled up, and as we entered the courtyard were immediately hit-up by the local youths hawking their products. By now, we'd all somewhat gotten used to this. Ignoring their sales pitches, we waded through the small group into the courtyard.

As we approached the house, we passed a bust of DuBois on top of a small pillar. Another small building was to the right, and the main building was straight ahead. We went inside and paid a small fee to enter. Our guide informed us that they charged you extra if you wanted to take pictures inside the building.

As we walked through the building, our guide described Dubois' life in Ghana. We learned that DuBois moved to Ghana at the age of 93 on the invitation of Ghanaian President Kwame Nkrumah[*] in 1961. He lived there until his death at the age of 95 in August 1963 on the eve of Martin Luther King's March on Washington.

We toured his personal library, which contained books from his various studies and interests. His collection included some of his wife's books as well as copies of his Harvard thesis. We then saw his bedroom, which we were told was also the room where he died. It had been converted into a room to display his personal affects. This included robes from several graduations, gifts from other countries and display cases that housed his timeless quotes.

We were then led outside where we went into the smaller building. This was where the honorable brother was buried alongside his wife's ashes. After originally deciding not to pay to take pictures, I changed my mind after seeing his tomb. Wakeelah agreed and decided to pay for both Monique and myself.

---

[*] Kwame Nkrumah (1909-1972) led Ghana's effort to become the first African country to gain its independence from European colonial (in this case British) rule. He was Ghana's first prime minister (1957-1960) and first president (1960-1966).

W.E.B. DuBois Tomb, Accra, Ghana

We took our pictures and walked back to the truck. After getting in, I felt a slight sense of disappointment in what I'd seen. Don't get me wrong, it was a tremendous honor and privilege to see where DuBois spent the last two years of his life, but the display was not worthy of a man as significant as he is to the black community and the world. For a brother with that kind of stature, this display was booty.

The property was kind of run down. Our guide was handling DuBois' books with his bare hands. I asked him if these books had been preserved. He replied "No". I thought, what the hell are you doing handling these books so carelessly? I was sure some that some of them were still in print, but he admitted that some of them weren't. No temperature control, no light control, it was like nobody gave a damn. I couldn't help but think, would other races let this happen to their heroes? For some reason, I didn't think so.

Dr. Maulana

We left the DuBois center and went to the Nkrumah Memorial in downtown Accra. As we pulled up to the memorial, we ran into one of Ba-

51

Ba's friends, Dr. Hamet Maulana. Dr. Maulana was a history professor at the University of Ghana and was a leader of the Reparations and Repatriation Effort for African-Americans. He told us about his plans for a conference in Accra to discuss the Reparations effort.

In just a few minutes, he impressed me as a powerful brother with a ton of energy. He told us that he had a duty to educate his fellow "Diasporans". He also mentioned that he wanted to meet with us, and he would rearrange his schedule to do so. We told him that Monday evening would be best and just like that, he agreed.

We said our goodbyes and moved towards the Nkrumah Memorial. After double-checking our itinerary, we knew we had to be mindful of a dinner engagement with one of Wakeelah's friends later in the day. If we spent too much time at the memorial, we knew it would make us late. So we decided to check out Labadi Beach instead and come back later to see the memorial. We didn't want to rush through such an important site.

Labadi Beach

On the way to the beach, Ba-Ba told us that the beach was located where the "La" people were from. He also mentioned that the term "Labadi" was a derogatory term used by colonialists to describe the "bad" La people. Somehow, the term stuck and was still in use today.

Yao drove us to the beach where we again paid a small fee to enter. As soon as we stepped toe on the beach, we were swarmed. First, by this tall dark skinned brother with two small diamonds in his front teeth. He was cool though. Providing a brief respite from the gathering crowd, he brought us over to his sister's bar for a quick tour. We dapped each other up, and Lavelle took a picture with him. She thought he was cute.

From there we moved towards the water and the beach. No one in our party had on bathing suits and I noticed that not many others did either. We took a few steps on the beach, and we were again approached.

Rastas, children, teenagers, grown men and women, they all clamored for our attention. These kids made the most high-pressure sales person in the States seem tame. Many of them were pushing goods in our faces, begging us to buy. I didn't mind a brother trying to make a Cedi, but damn!!! Sometimes you felt like saying "Would you please back the FUCK up?!?" The beach proved to be a strong test of my self-control.

While we were being swarmed, a brother with a horse came up and offered us a ride for a small fee. Lavelle decided to take him up on his offer. She hesitated getting on the horse, and brother man said he would pick her up. Before you could ask "What?" he picked her up and put her on the horse. Needless to say we were both impressed.

Lavelle at LaBadi Beach

Lavelle rode for a little bit while the rest of us tried to walk down the beach. Wakeelah was handling them like a pro, while Monique and I struggled to enjoy the beach. One dark skinned brother with a gravelly voice (think reggae singer Shabba Ranks mixed with rapper DMX) was especially persistent.

After a while, I eventually purchased something. Even though they bugged us, we all realized that we could get good deals down there. I ended up buying some bracelets, an Oware game, a mask, a jewelry box and some other gifts for my family and friends.

I decided to purchase my remaining gifts at a more relaxed location. These public areas were highly charged and were sometimes overwhelming. We were all shocked to hear mild-mannered Monique go off on someone at the beach. Wakeelah even had to school some young brother who had disrespected her.

We eventually left the beach and went back to Hibiscus to wash-up and change for dinner with Lucy, one of Wakeelah's friends. Lucy was dedicated to empowering sisters and rebuilding Ghana through entrepreneurship.

Lucy

Once we got back to Hibiscus, we showered, got dressed and met in Wakeelah's room. We received word that Lucy had sent her son Samuel to pick us up. While we were waiting in Wakeelah's room, we got pulled into a movie on TV about a woman who was beating up her fiancée and eventually killed him. I thought I had seen it before and I explained what I could remember about its ending so we could leave.

It wasn't long before Samuel had arrived and we were downstairs greeting him. He drove us to his house, which was only about 10 minutes away. The house was what we would describe as middle-class. His dad was in the living room watching the European Cup Soccer tournament. As in most non-American countries, soccer was big in Ghana. Samuel's dad gave us another warm Ghanaian welcome and asked us to sit. The maid came out to serve us water. He explained that his wife had stepped out for the moment but would return shortly. We talked about politics, his wife and sports. We all commented on how young he looked for being almost 70.

About an hour passed before Lucy finally came in. She was a short, brown-skinned woman with short hair and cute glasses. Her voice vaguely resembled my mother's. She immediately impressed me as an energetic woman who was about making a real difference in Africa. I'll say this about Wakeelah's friends in Africa, they definitely weren't faking the funk. They believed in what they were doing and appeared to be serious about rebuilding Africa. This was in contrast to some of the folks you see back home. Oftentimes, you'll hear a brother talking about "I'm about this" or "I'm about that" and they ain't about shit. Of course, Wakeelah's friends could turn out to be no different. Hopefully they won't fall into that category.

Lucy began to talk to us about her frustrations in dealing with the Ghanaian government and how corruption was at an all-time high. She described how the government foolishly gave away their rights to many of the country's natural resources. This in turn created a situation where only a few crooked politicians benefited while the masses suffered. Ghana, in her opinion, should be a powerhouse on the world stage given its vast resources.

Lucy also told us about the difficulties she faced when she planned her Women Entrepreneuers meeting in Miami in the spring. Yes, Elian* messed that up too. Her featured speaker was somehow tied up with that mess and didn't show up. She felt that Miami was basically Cuba North and that blacks seemed to cower in the background while Cubans took over.

---

* Elian Gonzalez was the young boy at the center of an international tug-of-war between the U.S. and Cuba.

Eventually, we moved to the dinner table for a meal of red snapper, rice and spinach with barracuda. The food was off the hook! During dinner, we talked some more about her philosophies and I commented to myself that this woman made a lot of sense. I began to think, "You know what happens to outspoken leaders when they make too much sense. Duck."

After we finished dinner, she continued to remind me of my mother by offering us more to eat. She even looked like my mom a little. I guess that meant I was missing her.

We eventually moved back to the living room where I took a seat in a chair with my back facing the front door, which was open. Given my earlier thoughts on what usually happens to folks who try to buck the system, this made me feel uneasy. I kept wondering if there was a sniper outside about to bust me in my head with a hollow point bullet for associating with Lucy. I subconsciously slid down in the chair, thinking that its plushy cushions would somehow protect me from harm.

Lucy's young daughter Nina was in the living room. She had changed the channel to a European soap opera. I was actually hoping we could catch the Tyson fight that was scheduled to come on that evening. Nina told us that she was going to high school in Canada. That's right, Canada. It was funny, when you listened to Nina speak, you could hear a Caucasian accent. Very strange hearing that in the middle of all that Black Power. She seemed real nice though.

We took some pictures, exchanged email addresses and prepared to leave. They gave us warm hugs and had Samuel drive us back to the hotel. On the way, Samuel and I talked about his plans to study computers in the U.S. I told him to look me up when he got to the States.

We arrived at Hibiscus and decided to gather in my room for the Tyson fight. We ordered ice cream and ate some more of those double chocolate chip cookies. Wakeelah had her dessert and shortly thereafter went back to her room. She was so tired she had little interest in the fight.

Monique had her dessert, read some of my journal, and soon followed Wakeelah upstairs, another victim of fatigue. Lavelle stayed and watched the Tyson fight with her little bro. The fight was over in 38 seconds with Tyson knocking the guy out. Oh well, so much for that. At least we didn't pay to see this debacle.

I needed to go to bed but my stomach was full of red snapper, barracuda and freezer-burned ice cream. Basically, it was going to be a while before I could nod off. I knew I was going to be fighting sleep when we had our 7:00 AM meeting with the Obodi chief.

Sunday, June 25, 2000

Meeting The Obodi Chief

After only a couple of hours of sleep, I surprisingly woke up at 6:00 AM. I called Lavelle to make sure she was up, but her line was busy. I figured she must have already been up, so I didn't worry about her. While I was in the bathroom, my phone rang. It was Lavelle, calling to make sure I was up. She sounded groggy, but I let her know that I was getting ready. I jumped in the shower, then started to get dressed. While getting ready, the phone rang again. This time, it was Wakeelah, sounding a little perturbed. She told me that my sister told her I just woke up. This was around 6:30 AM, and she was worried because we needed to be at the chief's palace by 7:00 AM. Standing in my underwear, I told her to give me five minutes. Staying true to my word, I was ready and outside in five minutes.

Wakeelah, Yao and Monique were already in the lobby. Lavelle arrived shortly thereafter, looking pissed. Apparently, there was some confusion regarding Wakeelah's earlier call to Lavelle. Wakeelah said it was a wake-up call, while Lavelle said Wakeelah just wanted to know what time it was, which was around 5:00 AM. Lavelle hung up and slept until 6:00 AM, while Wakeelah got ready. Well, there was tension in the air because we were again running late, and no one wanted to be blamed for making us late to our first meeting with the Obodi chief.

We got in the truck. Very few words were spoken as we drove to Ba-Ba's house to pick him up. Once in the truck, Ba-Ba could sense that something was amiss, because we were so quiet. When he asked us what was wrong, someone mentioned how tired we were, and the conversation moved on from there.

Yao took us straight to the Chief's house. We arrived at the front gate 12 minutes late and feeling a bit edgy. We weren't sure how the chief would respond to our tardiness. We went around to a side gate where Ba-Ba got out of the truck to knock. A young girl answered and gestured for us to come in. When we got out of the truck, we noticed the many cattle that the chief owned. Several dogs were in the yard as well.

We made our way to the same veranda where we sat the day before. The young maid brought out water for everyone and told us the chief would be with us shortly. While we waited, Ba-Ba described the medicinal properties of local trees, while a male servant swept up stray leaves in the courtyard. After a short time period, the chief appeared. He was a short man who looked a lot like Joe Frazier. He had the whitest teeth. Many of the Ghanaians that we'd seen had beautiful smiles, despite all of the poverty. Someone needed to do a study and mass-produce whatever it was that made everyone's teeth so nice.

To show our respect, we all stood as the chief greeted us. We shook his hand and then took our seats. He was dressed casually, in a striped shirt and Capri pants. He sat back comfortably in his chair. Ba-Ba began to tell him about who we were and the purpose of our visit. When you visited people in Ghana, especially chiefs, the tradition was to explain your "mission" or the purpose of your visit.

Ba-Ba told them about how my sister and I were looking for our roots. The chief confirmed what Ba-Ba and Yao had mentioned to us earlier about our family, specifically the origin of the Matey's and the Krobos.

We also talked about Wakeelah's husband, whom the chief fondly remembered. We talked some more about violence in America and how it had really gotten out of control.

The chief asked us if we would like to pour libations. Since it was tradition, we agreed. He disappeared into the house for a moment and emerged with a bottle of Schnapps. It seemed that the British came in a while back and introduced this drink to the Ga people. This somehow got worked into the libation ritual. The chief also had sodas brought out for the non-drinkers.

The chief took the Schnapps and poured it into a glass. He then poured some of it on the ground, drank the rest and passed the glass down. Ba-Ba was next. The servant poured the Schnapps, and he repeated the ritual. Wakeelah did the same. Then the glass was passed to me. Even though I'm generally a non-drinker, I went ahead and repeated the ritual, fearful of looking soft in front of the chief.

Lavelle and Monique chose sodas, while Yao chose the alcohol. After we'd all gone around, we sat for a few more minutes. We then left the chief so he could get ready for church. He invited us to come back on Tuesday so we could meet other members of the Ga-Obodi tribe.

We got into our vehicle and drove off. We stopped briefly at Ba-Ba's house, where Lavelle, Wakeelah and I went to use the bathroom. The house had a cozy feel to it. I talked with Ba-Ba about what we discussed with the chief. I also learned more about Ba-Ba's other activities and looked at a picture of his wife, who was not home at the time. We exchanged our contact information before we left. Ba-Ba decided to come with us so he could get a ride to New Achimota where he wanted to visit a friend.

On the way, we passed through the University of Ghana. It was a nice looking campus, but we didn't get a chance to stop and take pictures. This area looked more developed than the areas that we had seen earlier. We passed by some small shops and through a golf course, the first one I'd seen since being in Ghana. We then reached New Achimota where we dropped off Ba-Ba before going back to Hibiscus for breakfast.

Service at the Guest House

At Hibiscus, we went to the dining room and placed our breakfast orders. Overall, the place looked wonderful and the staff was pleasant. The only drawback was they didn't seem to have enough staff. Since we'd been there, the rooms had never been turned-over, our laundry was late and the food service was sometimes very slow. The workers were a bit overwhelmed because during our stay, they were preparing to host two large birthday parties over the upcoming weekend. Since the workers were getting ready for the parties, we had become secondary. Also, the owner of the guesthouse was away in Liberia on business. You know what they say happens when the cat's away.

Anyway, we waited for over an hour for our breakfast to come. Keep in mind we were the only four people in the dining room. I know, I know, you're probably thinking "impatient Americans." But I think by anyone's standards, an hour is too long for what we ordered. It was so bad that Wakeelah offered to return to Hibiscus in the fall to give free training sessions to the staff.

Anxiety Sets In

Eventually, our food arrived. We ate and then headed back to the rooms. Lavelle and I were waiting for Mrs. Hayford to meet us so we could meet the rest of our family. We were both a little apprehensive because we didn't know what to expect. For some reason, a sense of calm came over me and I began to think that somehow, everything was going to be just fine.

Dansomah

My sister and I went back to my room where we relaxed and awaited Mrs. Hayford's arrival. She finally arrived at Hibiscus at around 1:45 PM. She was just coming from church and she looked beautiful, in a matronly kind of way. Her mother and two daughters were in the car.

Everyone in the car was decked out in their Sunday's best. We summoned Yao and asked him to bring up the truck since we planned on following Mrs. Hayford. Monique decided to stay in her room because she was not feeling well, and with us not knowing what to expect, she didn't want to risk getting sicker.

We left Hibiscus and soon entered what seemed to be heavy traffic for a Sunday afternoon. Yao diligently followed Mrs. Hayford's car and we soon ended up in a town called North Kanesh. This city looked a little more modern than some of the other cities we'd been through. The neighborhoods had a suburban feel to them. You saw houses with gates topped with sharp thorns or broken glass intentionally set in concrete to discourage intruders.

Mrs. Hayford pulled into an old looking apartment building. We were told these buildings were constructed when Nkrumah was in office. I had originally thought we'd reached our cousins' house. When we pulled up next to her car, Mrs. Hayford told us that she wanted us to meet her father, and that he lived in the building. Mrs. Hayford, Lavelle, Wakeelah and myself got out to go and meet her dad. We trudged up four flights of stairs to the top floor, past some laundry hanging in the hall and a young woman pounding fufu*. Poor Wakeelah was lagging behind as her knee had been bothering her since our hike through the rain forest.

We finally reached her father's apartment. He was a medium sized brother who seemed very happy to see us. His apartment felt a little cramped, but it was neat. We shook hands and hugged before he asked us to sit down. Mrs. Hayford introduced us and briefly told him about our visit. We looked at pictures of my Uncle Frankie and his family (my Aunt Rebecca, cousins Lenny and Lorraine). We conversed a bit before we got up and went back downstairs. I'd say our total visit was about 15 minutes. I'm sure Wakeelah thought she could have stayed in the truck and saved her knee since the visit was so short.

We trooped back downstairs and got back in our vehicles. Now we were going to our family's house in Dansomah. Mrs. Hayford maneuvered in and out of traffic. It wasn't long before a few cars separated us. Before you knew it, Mrs. Hayford zoomed through a traffic light, leaving us behind at the red. After hesitating, Yao decided to run the red light. Unfortunately, that moment of delay caused him to lose sight of Mrs. Hayford's car.

Yao eventually drove to a spot where he thought their car would pass and parked, hoping they would see us on the side of the road. We were all inside the truck feeling a bit miffed, wondering how in the world they'd find us. We briefly discussed alternative plans on trying to locate them before we decided to just stay where we were for a few minutes.

As we waited, I again noticed Ghana's bustling streets. We sat and watched two small boys pass our truck, arguing about carrying a heavy bag.

---

* fufu – a traditional African Dish.

Local youths rapped and hung out on the corner. More folks passed by, on their way home from church as cars buzzed up and down the street.

We waited for about 15 minutes before they finally passed by and saw us. Yao cranked up the engine and soon we were following them again.

We rode for several more minutes before we reached the town of Dansomah. The roads were unpaved and pretty soon had us bouncing again. The road jostled us so thoroughly that they should be considered by the amusement parks as some kind of new ride. We rode down a road that had some rough looking houses on the left and some nicer looking homes on the right. I prayed that she didn't turn left. Mrs. Hayford turned right, and we followed.

We reached the house and pulled up to the gate. A small woman opened the gate and motioned for Yao to pull his truck into the driveway. He did so and we got out of the vehicle. I was excited, thinking that we would finally get a chance to meet the cousins my mother always talked about.

The Boateng Clan

My heart was pumping as we went up the walkway. Once inside, we were greeted with hugs and hardy handshakes. I kept thinking, wow, these folks helped raise my mother. My mother's cousin Rosina and my Great Aunt Dora greeted us. She gave each of us a big hug. The family patriarch, Mr. Boateng, also greeted us. He was a soft-spoken man who seemed to relish his role as the family leader. I could only hope that one day I'd be as blessed as he was.

We all sat down and talked for a bit. Everyone seemed genuinely happy that this occasion had finally arrived. I looked around and felt very comfortable in the house. Through the back windows, you could see another house just behind the main house. This was the family complex where several generations lived together as one big family.

To celebrate the joyous occasion, someone asked for a prayer to be said. After looking around at each other, Mrs. Hayford stepped up. She led us in a beautiful prayer and song that brought Wakeelah and Lavelle to tears. When she finished, we all said a heartfelt amen and continued to count our blessings. Soon afterwards, Mrs. Hayford left for another engagement. As she walked through the door, she jokingly told us that she had to report to her brother-in-law (my uncle Frankie) that we'd arrived safely.

As was tradition, drinks were soon offered. Other family members began to trickle into the living room so we could meet them. We met the entire family.

Papa

Rosina along with her brothers Papa and Christian remained with the elders and the rest of the adults. As we talked, I kept looking at Papa, my mother's favorite cousin. In a strange way, I felt connected to him. My mother and I had always had a close relationship. She and I were alike in demeanor and habits. Growing up she had mentioned her cousin Papa, and how much fun they used to have. Now here I was sitting right next to him. He seemed to have an easy-going temperament and I could immediately see why he and my mother got along.

James, Johannes "Papa" Boateng, Sandra, Emerald Boateng at the Boateng Residence, Dansomah, Ghana

The Family History

It wasn't long before we started asking questions about our heritage, discussing the information that we'd gathered on our trip. They confirmed everything that we'd been told by others about our family. They also told us

61

that my mother and her siblings were born in Odumase. Yao helped dig out more family secrets and helped by writing down everything that he heard.

He used his command of the language to really get the information we needed. He noticed that I was chatting with Papa and was too distracted to write the information down myself. Papa was telling me that he was leaving in the morning for a 14-hour drive to Kulungugu, a city at the northern border of Ghana. Papa, who was an architect, was to design a checkpoint station at the border.

Papa stepped out for a moment while the rest of us continued to talk. Mr. Boateng pulled out photos of he and Auntie Dora's 50th wedding anniversary in 1997. We commented on how blessed they'd been. We all wanted to get a family photo, so we gathered everyone around a beautiful bush with red flowers by the front porch.

Someone went to get Papa, who had gone to find some old photo albums. When he returned, he presented the photo albums with pictures of Lavelle and myself when we were young. Everyone laughed, including Yao. Wakeelah served as the group photographer and she got everyone in place. She took our picture and I thought about what a nice moment this was.

Lavelle (third from left) and James (fourth from left) with the Boateng Clan, Dansomah, Ghana

I took a few more individual photos and hugged my family members. My great aunt gave me a big, rocking bear hug and told us we'd better call her when we got back to the States. Wakeelah made Papa promise to look out for Lavelle and I with potential investments in Ghana.

Reluctantly we got into the truck, but not before we confirmed plans for another meeting with them on Tuesday. We exchanged contact information and left for Hibiscus. In the truck, everyone seemed happy and pumped, even "uncle" Yao. On this day, he and Wakeelah had become sort of honorary members of the family. We rearranged our schedule for the next day so we could go to Odumase and Dodowa after our meetings in the morning. I was definitely looking forward to going to my mothers' old stomping grounds.

Back at the Guest House

We arrived at Hibiscus House at around 6:00 PM. As we pulled up, we were serenaded by the sounds of Timbaland and Ginuwine's "Same Ol' G" booming from the outdoor speakers set up in the yard. Tonight was the second party being held at the house for the weekend. Two women were celebrating their 21st birthdays, so we were definitely expecting to see a young crowd. I had to admit, hearing the music really sounded good. I realized I was starting to miss home.

As we walked towards the door from the truck, I hugged Wakeelah and thanked her for her leadership and coordination of this trip. She had helped create lasting moments in our family history. Lavelle came over and did the same. We hung outside for a minute and observed the last minute preparations before going in to wash up for dinner.

While we changed for dinner, the power went out, causing some concern for the partygoers. It seemed like the extra stereo equipment overloaded the circuits. It stayed dark for about 15 minutes before the power was restored.

NaNa Kow

Hungry from the day's adventures, it wasn't long before we made our way to the dining area. Just before dinner, we were sitting with Wakeelah's herbalist, NaNa Kow. He seemed like another interesting brother who was into astrology, numerology and mysticism. Our conversation ranged from "cosmic vibrations" to Santana to homosexuality. It sounds weird, but he was really making sense. I guess anything could make sense when you're hungry.

Learning about the Armstrongs

Dinner was finally served. This time, I ordered white rice, fried fish and vegetables. While we ate, we told Monique about our family experience. Afterwards, she revealed her sadness surrounding her own family's inability to make the type of connection we just had with our family. Issues regarding skin color and racial self-hatred still heavily plagued her family as it did many others. It's the age-old issue where her lighter skinned family members thought of themselves as better than their darker skinned relatives, and this obviously caused bitter feelings. After hearing her explain all this, it didn't seem like there was much hope for the older generation in her family.

We all encouraged her to lead the charge and break this cycle of hatred in her family so that going forward a new precedent could be set. She agreed, and we finished our dinner.

More on NaNa Kow

Before we left the dining area, we talked to NaNa Kow about various ailments. He was very knowledgeable and came across as very easy going. He was a small man who looked to be about 35, but as we talked we discovered he was actually 52. He advised us as we wearily walked back towards our rooms where the party was in full swing. We finally reached the gates where we said goodbye to NaNa Kow before joining the party. The booming music seemed to be calling us and had temporarily revived our tired bodies.

Party Over Here

The music was pumping, but most of the guests were seated on the lawn while the dance floor, which was actually the main driveway, remained empty. Wakeelah decided to grab four small boys and ushered them to the dance floor. She was having fun. Monique, Lavelle and I danced in place for a while and talked. Before you knew it, more and more people got up to dance.

A young brother who wanted to dance soon approached Wakeelah. She agreed and was again grooving to some miscellaneous hip-hop beat. We all stood back and wondered why Wakeelah had a pained expression on her face. Perhaps her knee was bothering her, I thought. When she returned, she told us about brother man, or should I say that Kool and the Gang, 70's funk body odor he hit her with. Wakeelah described how she felt like she was being hit across the face with funk with every dance move. She was doing the rope-a-dope[*] trying to avoid the funk.

Wakeelah dancing with a "strong" young brother, Hibiscus Guest House, Accra, Ghana

As she finished her description, he came over and asked Lavelle to dance. He was all up on her. They danced, danced, danced and we laughed, laughed, laughed at her futile attempts to get off the dance floor and out of the funk. When he stepped away for a moment, I tried to save my sister by stepping in to dance with her. But somehow, he maneuvered his way back into Lavelle's face. I moved towards the edge of the dance floor, defeated by the funk. Lavelle languished for a while longer before she finally broke away.

---

[*] rope-a-dope – boxing technique used by Muhammad Ali where he leaned back on the ropes to avoid being hit.

After a few more songs, he returned again. The ladies were like, "Brother, please". He didn't understand English very well, but he did utter one word, "address." He wanted our addresses. Even at a nice little socialite party like this, people were still looking for sponsors. When you looked at the crowd, you could see desperation mixed in with the privileged few.

There was one table set up on the outskirts of the parking lot where some poorly dressed, tattered looking people were seated. Whoever organized the party must have felt obligated to invite these folks, but the line of separation was clearly drawn. The remote location of their table seemed to say, "You can dance, maybe even get some chop, but keep your ass away from us". Meanwhile, the socialites were seated on the nicely manicured lawn along with a host of 19 to 23 year olds.

Dancing Queen

In the middle of the dance floor was a pretty, petite young woman dressed in a beautiful Kente outfit with a head wrap. She was dancing by herself and it definitely didn't bother her. As the DJ played Will Smith's "Gettin' Jiggy Wit It", she proceeded to do just that by working those hips. This sister could dance, and her movements showed authority and confidence. She looked like she was having fun. It turned out she was one of the two birthday girls celebrating that night. She danced while others grooved around her.

Later that evening, our group ended up talking to her. She told us her name was Regina. It was funny because she pronounced her name with a hard "i", so with the blaring music, you know what that sounded like to me. She's lucky I generally don't drink. Anyway, the ladies split off and I was left talking with Regina.

Birthday Girl, Regina at Hibiscus Guest House, Accra, Ghana

She had a pleasant, effervescent personality. She smiled a lot and was very touchy-feely which of course I didn't mind. I decided to flirt a little bit. I figured what the hell, I might as well have some fun. I started rapping, hitting her with that D.C. flavor and savoir faire. I was also trying to figure out her angle. By the way she was talking, I knew sooner or later it was coming. "What's your address?" I was like, damn, you too? I was hoping I could get her to sponsor me! Eventually, I gave her my e-mail address. I figured if she got annoying, I could always hit "delete."

67

August, My Man

In the meantime, I went over to speak with one of the guys who worked at Hibiscus, George August. I always referred to him as "August, My Man" in a fake British accent because he usually was so serious and refined. Not tonight. He and Yao were tipsy and feeling a buzz. The three of us ended up sitting all over the car of the birthday girls' father. Yao was actually stretched out across the hood of the man's car, looking quite disheveled. Basically, we were straight ghetto.

George August and Yao, enjoying the party

Big Sista Wakeelah

Wakeelah noticed how tacky this looked and playfully persuaded us to get off the man's car. Soon afterwards, I went to get drinks for myself and the crew. I tried to get three sodas from the cooler in the party, and a woman started going off. She mentioned that she purchased the sodas at the party and that she didn't want any outsiders, meaning us, getting free drinks.

Gifti, one of the cooks at Hibiscus, was serving as a hostess. She quietly led me away as I balanced the sodas in my hands. As I walked, I felt that sister's glare burning a hole in the back of my head. Not wanting to cause a problem, I went back and offered to pay for the sodas. Gifti continued to tell me not to worry about it, and I went back to our crew.

I proceeded to tell them the story. The first thing Wakeelah asked was "Where is she?" in a tone that let you know she wanted to kick somebody's ass. It seemed like the Great Communicator had not forgotten how to throw down. I was waiting for her to pull out a jar of Vaseline for her face.

Acting like a sister protecting her little brother, Wakeelah asked me to give her the money I offered to the lady. We went around the corner and she said, "Point her out." As we rounded the corner, the woman had her back to us, still arguing about the sodas. As we approached, she stood back, looking like she didn't know what was going to happen.

She saw me first, then I stepped to the side and she saw Wakeelah. She turned away slightly, probably thinking she was about to get bitch-slapped in front of her people. Wakeelah grabbed the woman's hand, placed the money in it and sarcastically said, "Sister, we don't want to look like we're crashing your party. We want to pay for the sodas."

Expecting her to say something like, "Oh no, don't worry" or "It's OK", I was a little surprised to see her grip the money and say "Thank you!" in a tone that let you know she was pissed.

Wakeelah and I were again led away by Gifti before things got ugly. We went back to our group and described what happened. We laughed because we knew we wouldn't really have resorted to violence to solve the problem but it was fun acting like badasses who wouldn't take any shit.

Pure Silliness

Eventually, we all congregated in Lavelle's room. We talked about our friends and their views on Africa before we started to laugh and act silly. We laughed even harder when Wakeelah told the story of how the inebriated pair of Yao and August were staring at her like a piece of meat earlier in the evening. She said they had that glassy, glazed look in their eyes as they looked her up and down.

She also mentioned how Yao tended to "grab himself" every time someone agreed with him about something, as if to say, "Damn straight!" Seeing Wakeelah imitate this movement was hilarious. Monique had even taken to imitating this move. Again, this was too funny.

Eventually, we decided to go back downstairs to see if Yao was still laid out across the car. When we got downstairs, the crowd had thinned out. Only a few people remained. In the hall, we ran into Kwasi, another worker at Hibiscus. He was like the Mr. Everything at Hibiscus, because he seemingly did it all. Cooking, cleaning, laundry, sewing, you name it, he did it. We joked with him and complimented him on the abada he made for himself. We laughed and joked some more before giving him our clothes to iron in the morning.

James Gaines

As I was leaving, Regina the birthday girl happened to be standing next to our group talking to someone else. She stopped me and asked me if she'd be able to reach me at Hibiscus later on in the week. I told her we were there until Wednesday. She got all giggly and smiled, and after a few more words, I told her good night. I·turned to say a few more words to my group before finally heading to my room. As she left, she passed behind me and brushed her hand across my back. Why did I think this wouldn't be the last time I'd hear from her?

Monday, June 26, 2000

Dog Tired

It was 6:00 AM and the phone startled me out of my sleep. I was extremely tired because I had been up late writing in my journal. I think I only got about two hours of sleep and my head was killing me. I got up and made my way down to the small dining area where Kwasi and the other workers sometimes slept. The night before, Kwasi told me he would have my clothes ironed and dropped off at my room by 6:00 AM.

As I reached the dining area, I saw Kwasi and the other workers asleep in various parts of the room. The guys looked worse then I felt. Maybe they had partied a little too hard because they were seriously dragging ass. Kwasi, always overworked, sheepishly begged for my forgiveness and told me how tired he was. Hearing this, I modified my request and asked him to just knock the wrinkles off of my pants. As I walked back to my room, I remembered that they still hadn't finished my laundry from several days ago.

I got back to my room to get ready for the day. Since everything seemed to be running slow that morning, we all called our breakfast orders in around 7:00 AM, hoping they'd be ready for us by the time we walked over.

Lavelle, Monique and myself eventually gathered in the lobby and walked over to the dining house. Wakeelah had already walked over. On the way, we saw Yao looking a little rushed. He greeted us and reached out to shake our hands. Each of us was a little hesitant, knowing that shaking hands with Yao meant having to wash them all over again because we had never seen him wash his hands during our various experiences in Ghana. We all shook and confirmed our departure time of 8:00 AM.

We walked over and sat down with Wakeelah. My head was really hurting and I was not talking much. We waited 10, 15, 20, 30 minutes, still no food. And this was after ordering early. We were all getting impatient, knowing that if we didn't get the food in the next few minutes, we'd have to leave without it and what they were preparing would go to waste.

We told our server about our schedule, and she checked on the food again. Within a few minutes, the food arrived. We ended up scarfing down our meals because we knew we had to scoot. Today we were meeting with Vice Chancellor Addae-Mensah of The University of Ghana and of course, we did not want to be late.

We walked out to the carport, ready to jet, and Yao was nowhere to be found. Where the hell did he go this time? After repeatedly saying "we cannot be late", Wakeelah ended up getting another hotel worker to drive us to the meeting. This poor fellow came out in what looked like pajamas and got behind the wheel.

Traffic was kind of heavy, but it wasn't long before we reached the university. Once on campus, we stopped several times to ask for directions to the Vice Chancellor's office. We finally reached his office, about 20 minutes late. After a short wait in the lobby, we were escorted into the Vice Chancellor's office. We talked for a few minutes. I had very little to say since I was feeling irritable. Monique presented him with another MSU bowl, and before you knew it we were leaving. The VC had another meeting he had to get to, so we left with him.

As we walked out, Yao was sitting in the lobby waiting for us. I was too tired and too pissed off to say anything to him, so I kept walking. His disappearances were downright aggravating. Surprisingly, Wakeelah didn't get on his case for his latest episode. We got in the truck and headed to Odumase, my grandfather's hometown.

The Road to Odumase

The weather was sunny and warm. The roads that we were on were surprisingly paved and the views were cinematic. We passed through several towns that seemed to run together, including Madina Atomic Junction, Adenta, and then Dodowa. Dodowa was where my grandmother was from, so I sat up in my seat so I could take in the town. Getting a chance to view her hometown gave me a second wind.

Dodowa had lots of trees, bushes and low greenery. While we drove through, Bill Withers' "Lovely Day" played on the radio. We all sang along as we passed a beautiful mountain range covered with trees and shrubs. His song seemed to be the perfect soundtrack for this experience.

We eventually drove through a bustling section of Dodowa, passing a post office and a school. We also passed many mango trees and a market crowded with people. Yao explained that the market was very busy because Monday and Thursday were days when people did their heavy shopping in that area.

Lavelle and I asked Yao to pull over so we could take pictures. We took a picture at the Dodowa Presbyterian Primary School, along with some shots of the mountains and beautiful plant life.

As we continued to drive, the crowds of people were more spread out. Villages were not as populated as some of the earlier places that we'd seen.

We saw fields of maize, tomatoes and many other vegetables as we drove down miles of paved road with no traffic.

We eventually passed through Agomeda, where we saw more mountains, including "Shai Hill". Yao told us that this was where Krobos used to celebrate their Mayum Festival. They would give thanks for a bountiful harvest, similar to what Americans did for Thanksgiving. We were also told that this was the heart of Krobo country.

From Agomeda, we reached Somanya, another Krobo town. This city felt more congested than Agomeda. As we drove through, we passed through a swarm of bees that someone stirred up. That was a little eerie because they appeared to come out of nowhere in the middle of a busy street.

We eventually reached Odumase where we stopped briefly at the Krobo chief's palace. Yao got out to ask for directions to the Madjitey residence, home of my grandfather's people. We got the directions, and continued on our way.

Just outside of Odumase was the small town of Asite. We turned off the main road onto a dirt road and went about ¾ of a mile. We passed the tomb of the former police chief of Ghana Eric Madjitey, the man my mother referred to as "Uncle Police", my great uncle. He was the first police chief of Ghana under Nkrumah's rule. Even today, we found that his name commanded respect.

Tomb of my great uncle Eric R.T. Madjitey, first Head of Ghanaian Police Service

73

Soon, we reached the house. Yao and I walked up to the front entrance of the house and a young woman invited us in. Everyone else waited in the truck. Two elderly women were sitting on the couch talking quietly in the living room. When they saw us walk in, they pleasantly said, "You are welcomed. Please sit down". Now that was different. If two strange males had walked into a house in the States, "welcomed" was the last thing they would be asked to feel.

We took a seat, and Yao began to explain our mission. When he told them who I was, they looked at me and screamed with joy! They couldn't believe that their great nephew had come to visit. Yao went out to the truck to get everyone else.

We all hugged and kissed. The ladies turned out to be my great aunt Comfort, who was my grandfather's sister, and my great aunt-in-law Vera, who was married to "Uncle Police". Auntie Comfort cried, saying she had always prayed for this day.

We asked a lot of questions, trying to learn as much as we could about my grandfather's side. Vera did most of the talking while Auntie Comfort cried and shook her head in disbelief.

After we talked, Auntie Comfort and Auntie Vera led us on a tour of the grounds. We saw up close where my Great Uncle was buried, and we toured the Madjitey compound. The land was in disrepair, and Auntie Comfort explained that she was the last person left from my grandfather's generation. She had a son named Evans who worked in Tacqua and only came by on the weekends to help maintain what was left. Other than the three of them, that was it.

We couldn't keep up with Auntie Comfort as we toured the compound. She was ahead of us and pointed everything out. I hung back and helped Auntie Vera walk around. It was hot and the sun was unforgiving. Auntie Comfort told us how the land was ours if we wanted it. She begged us to come back and help take care of the land.

I always wondered why my mother never talked about this place or made any effort to come back. We knew something happened with my grandmother after my grandfather died, but we didn't know what. So far, no one tried to run us off when we said we were related to the Sikapa/Madjiteys. In fact it was quite the opposite reaction. Everyone seemed in awe, like wow, you're down with the Madjitey's? I figured that I would ask my mother about this when we got back to the U.S.

74

Sandra, Great Aunt Vera Madjitey, James, Unidentified Cousin, Great Aunt Comfort Sikapa, Asite, Ghana

We made our way back to the house to get out of the sun. Soft drinks were brought out to quench our thirsts. As we wrapped up our meeting, we took pictures and exchanged addresses. I asked Auntie Comfort to have her son contact me, especially after she revealed that he was the keeper of the Madjitey family history.

She also told me that some European had come down to get copies of the Madjitey family history to take back to Europe. I told Auntie that Evans must get in contact with me so we could talk. I wanted to get a copy of the history, and I also wanted to warn him to be careful not to get pimped by that European.

Before we left, we gave Auntie Comfort $40 as a small gift for everything that they'd done to maintain the grounds. We got in the truck and drove off. I left feeling mixed emotions. I was thrilled that I finally met relatives on my grandfather's side of the family, but I was sad that we couldn't stay longer. I hoped that one day I'd be able to return.

As we turned down the windy roads of Asite and Odumase, we took pictures of the beautiful scenery. Some of this stuff looked like it was straight out of a Disney movie. It was that pretty.

Yao jumped on the Tema Motorway and we left for home. By then, it was early afternoon and the sun was hot. After being on the road for a few minutes, we all fell asleep. I woke up after about 20 minutes and noticed how this particular road looked like some of our highways back home.

7-11

We reached the guesthouse after about a 45-minute drive exhausted. We went up to Lavelle's room and started snacking on some wheat thins and lemon cookies that Monique brought with her. Monique had developed the reputation of being the most prepared person to ever travel. No matter what you needed, she had it. If you needed medicine, she had it. Food? She had it. Insect repellant? She had it. Juicy juice? SHE HAD IT. I started calling her "7-11" for obvious reasons.

After sitting in Lavelle's room for a few minutes, I went down to my room. Lavelle decided to follow, while Monique went to her room. I turned on the AC and changed clothes. Lavelle read my journal while I again nodded off.

By the time I woke up, Lavelle was gone. Yao stopped by my room as I had asked so I could confirm the family information we collected during the day. Yao was sometimes better at catching relevant details because he understood the language and I didn't. So I wanted to be sure I heard things correctly.

After Yao left, we went to dinner. On the way out, I ran into NaNa Kow. I told him about our journey, and he seemed pleased that we met more members of our family. He decided to walk over to dinner with us. On the way, he gave us more advice on health remedies.

That night, I had fried fish, jollof rice and vegetables, my standard meal at Hibiscus. We continued to chat with NaNa Kow.

We were expecting Mrs. Hayford to stop by after work, and we were also expecting Dr. Maulana. Neither of them made it, and we ended up talking to NaNa Kow all night.

The Numerologist

In addition to being an herbalist, NaNa Kow mentioned he was also a numerologist. At one point during our conversation, he wrote down everyone's birth date and started giving predictions. With Lavelle, he told her that he didn't see a significant other in her life for a while. He told Monique that there would be a period of stress in her life towards the end of the year. Then he got to me.

After writing down my information, he warned me to be careful of doing business with shady people to avoid being involved in a scandal. He also "saw" that I was having marital problems. After finding out my estranged wife's astrological sign, he told me I should be glad that she was out of my life, and that I would never be able to "tame" her.

I played it off, acting like it didn't phase me, but in reality, it did. I said I was looking for a sign on this trip, and this one was 10 feet tall with flashing lights.

We ended the evening by taking pictures and saying good-bye to NaNa Kow. I went to my room, shaking my head. After a few minutes, Monique called, asking me to come upstairs so we could decide who should get what gift before we all left. We all met in her room, divvied up the gifts, and broke for the night.

Tuesday, June 27, 2000

Surprise, Surprise

I received a 7:00 AM wake-up call from the front desk. After previous requests for wake-up calls went unfulfilled, I was surprised that I had finally received one. I felt well rested. I could hear someone out on the lawn with a lawn-mower cutting the grass. No machetes here. I called the kitchen to order my breakfast before getting up to shower.

I admitted to myself that NaNa Kow's predictions bothered me. Scandal? Be glad that my wife was out of my life? This was heavy stuff. I tried to put it out of mind and got dressed. I had to do some serious recycling of my clothes, since there was no dry cleaning near the hotel. ·

On this day, we were returning to meet the Ga-Obodi chief and his council. Before breakfast, I went down to check on my laundry. While I was waiting, Kofi, Kwasi, Richard and Theresa, all Hibiscus employees, were talking. They seemed rested and relaxed. Kwasi ran off to get my laundry. Could it be? Was my laundry really done? Or would I get another sack of mildewed clothes? I talked to Richard and Kofi for a minute. I also took a quick peek out the window and noticed that Yao's truck was there. Hopefully, we wouldn't have a repeat of the MIA scenario from the day before.

Kwasi returned with my clothes. They were ironed and folded. I couldn't believe it. Pleasantly surprised, I returned to my room to drop off my clothes and check on Lavelle. She was still getting dressed. Wakeelah stopped by my room and told me she was heading over for breakfast.

After we ate, we all got together and got in the truck. We were supposed to pick up NaNa Kow and Ba-Ba before going to the Chief's house.

Everyone remained quiet. Despite the good times we'd had, you could sense that folks were ready to go home. No one had the energy for another day of hopping all over Ghana. As we drove, you could tell it was going to be a hot one. The sun was beaming and there wasn't a cloud in the sky. We had been lucky with the infamous African heat up until the last few days. I guess it was too much to expect that we wouldn't at least get a taste of it.

We picked up NaNa Kow and Ba-Ba and went towards the chief's residence. While we drove, Wakeelah mentioned her concern when she heard that several flights out of Ghana had been cancelled, and that our flights may have been in jeopardy. Not good news for the travel weary crew.

We decided that the most prudent thing to do would be to go to the airport ahead of time to confirm our flights. No waiting until the last minute for us.

After our conversation regarding our flights, we reached the Obodi chief's house in what seemed like minutes. We entered the courtyard and walked towards our familiar veranda. To the left of the veranda was a circular grove surrounded by tall trees that provided a canopy for anyone sitting in the circle. On this day, the Obodi council was conducting a meeting in this outdoor conference room. A desk, a small lamp and several chairs were spread out in the circle. About 15 men from the Obodi council occupied the circle as they discussed Obodi business. They waved at us as we took our seats on the veranda.

Before we got to the veranda, several council members came over and provided us with seats from their circle. The servant also provided us with water while we waited to be invited to the circle.

After about 10 minutes, one of the councilmen came over and invited us to join the circle. We walked over and went around the circle to introduce ourselves. As we went around the circle, I noticed that one of the chairs was empty, as if it had purposefully been left vacant. We finally shook the last person's hand, and then we took our seats.

Once we were seated, three of the younger council members stood up to shake our hands a second time and formally welcome us on behalf of the tribe. The chief welcomed us and briefly told his council who we were. He mentioned the fact that Wakeelah's husband was an Obodi chief, and he also mentioned that Lavelle and I were Ga-Krobos related to former police chief Madjitey. I noticed a few eyes and ears perk up when this was said.

NaNa Kow acted as our spokesperson. He announced our mission, this time with more detail. We each introduced ourselves by name so the Obodi scribe could document who we were in the meeting minutes.

When NaNa Kow finished, the chief explained that one of their council members had just died and that's why they had an empty chair in the circle. They also explained that one of the elders was not able to attend the meeting because he was not feeling well.

After the chief finished, Wakeelah spoke on behalf of her husband, Wali. Wali was fortunate enough to have been able to trace his roots back to the Obodis. His family had a strong oral tradition that passed the Obodi name down from generation to generation. This allowed him to eventually find his people in Ghana. He was enstooled as an Obodi chief the previous year and lived with them for a short period of time until he returned to the U.S. for a family emergency. The council remembered Wali well.

Wakeelah mentioned how her husband desperately wanted to be back with the Obodis where he truly felt at home. As she conveyed these thoughts to the group, Wakeelah was overcome with emotions and began to cry. She felt blessed to be able to sit with her husbands' tribe and be accepted as one of them.

The chief acknowledged Wakeelah's thoughts and passed to her a picture of him to take back to her husband. Wakeelah also shared some pictures of her family with the council.

After everyone viewed the pictures, it was time to pour libations. This time, Wakeelah had purchased two bottles of Schnapps that we presented as gifts to the chief. I passed the bottles to NaNa Kow and he presented them to the chief on behalf of our group.

The Obodi Council and our crew, Accra, Ghana

A younger council member took the drinks from the chief while the chief retrieved a glass. The young brother stood in the middle of the circle, said a few words, and then opened the drink. He poured some out, then poured some for the chief. The chief poured some out of the glass, drank, and then passed the glass down. As before, we all repeated the ritual, even Lavelle. I was surprised. Monique however, stuck to her guns. She wasn't drinking after anybody, especially eight strangers.

After the libation ceremony, we all moved to the courtyard to take a group picture. Once we finished with the pictures, we went back to the circle, collected our belongings and said our goodbyes. I definitely felt good being welcomed by my fellow Ga tribesmen, even though they are Obodis and I was Krobo. The difference didn't seem to matter much.

We decided to pay our respects to the older council member who could not attend the meeting by going to see him. Wakeelah also wanted to see the property that had been given to her husband so she could take pictures. Two of the younger Obodi councilmen rode with us to direct us.

We arrived at the elder's home and found him sitting on his porch resting. We walked in, shook his hand and took a seat. The two younger Obodis then went around the circle and shook our hands on their elder's behalf, formally welcoming us to his home. I was amazed when they told me he was 92, because he looked younger than that, maybe 70ish. He moved slowly and seemed to be very tired, so we didn't stay long. We paid our respects and rolled out.

After we left the councilman's house, we dropped the Obodi council members off at the chief's house and went back to Ba-Ba's to change out of our dress clothes. I had forgotten to pack my tennis shoes, so I was unable to change. I was pissed because it was hot, and it's hard to look cool with sweat running down your back. We also wanted to call Mrs. Hayford since we had planned on seeing her later in the day. Before we left, we presented Ba-Ba with a gift for all of his help.

Keeping Our Fingers Crossed

After we changed, we left for the airport to confirm our tickets. We arrived at Kotoka International and went to a small, crowded room we were told was the confirmation office. We stood in a line for several minutes before Lavelle, Monique and I were able to confirm our flight. That was a relief for all of us, since we were all looking forward to getting back home. Since Wakeelah was flying on Lufthansa and not Ghana Airways like the rest of us, we had to go to the Lufthansa office in Accra.

We left the terminal, walking past a loud argument at the taxi stand. We found the truck and went downtown to confirm Wakeelah's ticket. After we got there and Yao parked, Wakeelah went inside while we sat in the truck and waited.

After about 20 minutes, Wakeelah returned to the truck with not so good news. She was on stand-by and would have to report to the terminal early to see if her flight had a seat for her. Wakeelah decided to keep a positive attitude about it and hope for the best. We all agreed that having this type of attitude was a lot better than worrying about the situation.

The Nkrumah Memorial

From the Lufthansa office, we took off in the direction of the Nkrumah Memorial. Finally, we would get to see Ghana's tribute for the man who meant so much to the country. As we drove through the city, you noticed that it felt like a metropolitan area as opposed to the smaller villages that we had visited before. Traffic was heavy.

As we waited at traffic lights, foot-merchants hovered around the sides of the truck. They were selling everything from hair trimmers, to maps, to food. Each merchant jockeyed for position to get your attention. Some even ran along side your car for a short distance, desperately holding up their goods. Everyone tried not to make eye contact, because if you did, they fought even harder for your attention. I was just hoping that no one got their toes run over since they were so close to the vehicles. Even with this, Monique eventually bought a shirt, as did Lavelle.

We finally arrived at the memorial where we paid a small fee to enter. The outside was spectacular. There was a towering bronze statue of Nkrumah pointing in the distance flanked by two huge fountains. The fountains had statues of kneeling horn players with water flowing from the horns. The landscaping was beautiful as well. Lavelle, Monique and I went in while Yao and Wakeelah stayed in the truck. They had both seen the memorial numerous times in the past. We walked through a group of school children to find spots to take pictures. We then went towards the mausoleum and took pictures of Nkrumah's tomb.

Kwame Nkrumah Memorial, Accra, Ghana

We walked towards the museum building, which housed the Nkrumah exhibit. It was a one-room building that appeared small on the inside. As we walked in, a gentleman at the desk nonchalantly told us where to start. The room had pictures of Nkrumah on the wall from his life as a private citizen as well as a world leader. It also had different artifacts from his life including his books, gifts from world leaders, even a coffin used to transport his body after he died.

As with the DuBois Center, I again came away with a feeling of disappointment after viewing the inside of the museum building. For a man who led the country to independence from colonial rule, a better job should have been done in preserving his legacy for all to see. The outside was great, but the inside looked as if it was haphazardly thrown together at the last minute. Many of the pictures didn't have labels or had labels that were peeling off. Some of the pictures were so high on the wall that you couldn't see the picture very well. The room was dimly lit with a faint urine smell in the air. Obviously, not as much thought went into the inside as the outside. My advice would be for them to get rid of that building all together if it's not going to be done correctly.

In a way, this museum was a microcosm of the entire country. Ghana's history was too rich and they had too many resources for their country be in the shape that it's in. I realized that the legacy of slavery along with European colonialism and political corruption had taken its toll on most of Africa. It's truly a shame because with all of the gold, bauxite, manganese, timber, cocoa as well as other products, Ghana should be a major player on the world stage. I didn't know enough about the political climate in West Africa, but I knew somebody was benefiting from all that Ghana had to offer, and it wasn't the Ghanaians.

We walked back to the truck to find Wakeelah and Yao buying ice cream from a vendor carrying her product on her head. The ice cream was a welcome relief because it was so hot. We all had at least one scoop, and I mean a small scoop. This lady did not believe in giving out generous portions. It had to be about a teaspoon of ice cream in a small, stale cone. We ate it up anyway, then got in the truck.

As we attempted to exit, someone who claimed to be a parking attendant stopped us. The attendant asked us to pay for parking, even though there was no sign indicating that parking wasn't free. We reluctantly paid. I hoped that it wasn't a scam and the money went towards improving the inside of the museum building.

The Cultural Center

After leaving the Nkrumah Memorial, we went to the Cultural Center. Upon arrival, we were relieved to see a sign that said "hawkers not allowed". After our experiences at LaBadi Beach and riding through traffic, we'd all had about enough of the aggressive sales tactics.

As we walked along the row of shops, you could see the Gulf of Guinea in the distance. The shops themselves were sort of cobbled together with wood, thatch and maybe some aluminum.

The Cultural Center had a flea market feel to it. Each store we passed had items that showed off the craftsman's skill. The artisans took great pride in their products and they seemed to work from sun up to sun down, stopping occasionally to eat or to talk to potential buyers. They were all very creative with what they did with wood. We saw wood shaped into Adinkra symbols, animals, furniture, and much more.

We eventually turned around and went back towards the centralized shopping area. Even though the first row of vendors had impressive items, they were all too big for me to carry back on this trip, so I went to find something more portable.

The main shopping area was crowded and hot. There were hundreds of small shops crammed together under a makeshift roof. As you walked past the shops, merchants constantly asked you to come into their shop. Some were more aggressive than others, but none were as aggressive as the foot-merchants we encountered on previous shopping trips.

Monique and Yao continued on while Wakeelah took a different route. Lavelle and I stayed together. We walked around the entire market before we settled on one particular vendor. Many of the vendors had the same items for sale for similar prices, so I figured one would be just as good as the other.

Lavelle and I pointed out a few items and started bargaining. While shopping in Ghana, we learned that you never accepted the first price offered by a merchant. Always cut their original offer in half and work up. They respected you for that and they were willing to bargain. Sometimes they would even barter or trade goods with you. I had one friend who went to Gambia and Senegal who told me he traded a pair of his underwear for some goods. I told him he was trifling. Oh well, at least he got what he wanted.

After negotiating our prices, we realized that we were again running behind schedule. It was after 4:00 PM and we still had to visit Mrs. Hayford at the bank before 5:00 PM. We wrapped up our shopping and headed toward the truck sweaty, but satisfied. We had finished the majority of our shopping and didn't have to fool with the merchants anymore.

Yao drove us towards the bank where we met Mrs. Hayford. She was dressed sharply as usual and looked like The Woman sitting in her office. Her office overlooked the main floor where the clerks worked.

We went into her office where she greeted us with big hugs. She had an assistant bring in sodas while we talked. You could tell it was going to be a late night for her. The bank was closed and people were still buzzing around like it was 10:00 AM.

We asked Mrs. Hayford if she could convert our American dollars to cedis for us. She agreed to do so and gave us excellent rates without charging us the normal fee. It was nice to know people in high places. We finished our drinks, hugged and kissed her, then jumped back in the truck.

Before we pulled out, I ran back in so I could call in our dinner order at Hibiscus. We all knew how notoriously slow food service could be at the guesthouse. We were supposed to have a second visit with my great aunt later that evening and we weren't sure if dinner was being served. Not wanting to take a chance, we figured we'd eat at Hibiscus so we'd have something on our stomachs. Negotiating in all that heat made us really hungry.

Finally back on the road, Yao fought through the evening rush hour and got us back to Hibiscus. We washed up and hurried down for dinner.

While we were eating, we received a call from my second cousin Rosina, asking if we were still coming. They had fixed a big dinner for us and everyone was waiting. Since the staff at Hibiscus had already cooked our food, we decided to eat half our food so we wouldn't piss them off. We remembered we still had another day to go before our departure and they were still cooking our meals.

We hurriedly finished our dinner and got ready to get in the truck. The only problem was that Yao was missing again. He had gone to chop. We were already late and this didn't help. After a few minutes, Yao showed up and we took off for Dansomah.

A Family Affair

Once we finally were on the road, we figured we'd get to my cousin's house in about 20 minutes. It was well after rush hour so the traffic couldn't be that bad, or so we thought. Within minutes we were caught in heavy traffic. This coupled with the shoddy roads turned a short trip into about a 45-minute drive. The only good thing about the longer drive was that I got a chance to fall asleep along the way. After a long day, I definitely needed the rest.

We finally reached the Boateng residence, two hours late. As Rosina opened the gate, we profusely apologized to her. We did not want to seem unappreciative of the effort the family made to make dinner for us. They didn't seem mad though, and if they were, they hid it well.

Rosina escorted us through the front door where the family greeted us. Two new faces were amongst the small crowd. My great uncles Ben and Bob had made the trip to see us.

Uncle Ben had a very gentle personality and seemed like he didn't have a care in the world. Uncle Bob was a little feistier, although it was harder to understand his words when he spoke. The two of them together looked like they would have made a great comedy team as they played off of each other's words.

My Great Uncle Ben Matey, Great Aunt Dora Boateng, Great Uncle Bob Matey

The food was already prepared and waiting to be eaten. I had fully expected that the family would have eaten already since we were so late and I was surprised to see that most of them hadn't because they were waiting for us. I really felt bad about this. Everyone's disappointment seemed to melt away once we sat down at the table. We ended up having a wonderful meal of fish, banku with sauce and yams. The food was fantastic. Even though we had eaten at Hibiscus a short time before, most of us had no problem eating again.

Auntie Dora was on "Plate Patrol" to make sure everyone had plenty to eat. She walked around the table and would playfully tease anyone claiming that they were full. You weren't full until SHE said you were full! I see where my mother got this habit. Everyone realized that it was all in fun and it was her way of showing her love by filling you up with good food.

Mystery Solved

While we were eating, we were surprised to see Papa come out and greet us. He was supposed to have left on a road trip to northern Ghana for his job. He decided to postpone his departure to the next day so he could see us. That was cool, because we all enjoyed talking to him.

After dinner, we all moved to the sitting room for conversation and pictures. My great uncles and I talked and laughed a lot. Papa steered our conversation towards more serious matters when he talked about his disappointment in the way Ghana had not developed the way it should have for a country with so many resources. I had heard this thought echoed several times during my trip and I realized how frustrated many Ghanaians were with the country. Wakeelah and Auntie Dora stayed at the table and talked, while Yao fell asleep in the chair. Since he was doing all the driving, we let him get his rest.

While talking with Auntie Dora, Wakeelah found out what the riff was that caused my grandmother to leave her late husband's land. It seemed that Auntie Comfort and my grandmother never got along. Apparently, Auntie Comfort didn't think my grandmother was good enough for her brother, so she harbored ill will towards her. When my grandfather died, there was more strife and Auntie Comfort all but forced my grandmother to leave the family compound in Asite. My grandmother ended up leaving the land, vowing never to return. The way they treated my grandmother caused a bitter divide between Auntie Comfort and my grandmother's side of the family. According to Wakeelah, Auntie Dora was still upset about the whole thing. I guess some old wounds never heal.

After the heavy meals and the long day, everyone started to show their fatigue. We decided to get ready to hit the road. Auntie Dora surprised Lavelle and I with small necklaces. We then packed up some food that Lavelle and I planned on taking back home to mom.

Tonight's goodbye was harder than the one after our first visit. Since we knew that it would be a while before we returned, I made sure to hug everyone extra hard, and told them how much I enjoyed meeting them. I also promised to keep in touch with everyone. Auntie Dora gave me the strongest hug out of everyone, saying "Don't forget to call me when you get home!"

We all got in the truck, waved farewell, and drove into the night. Since it was late, we agreed to drop Uncle Bob and Uncle Ben at their respective houses. After a slight change of plans, we dropped my Uncle Bob off on a corner at a busy intersection, and then dropped Uncle Ben off at a crowded bus stop a few minutes later. After seeing them off, we finally left for Hibiscus.

Wednesday, June 28, 2000

The Final Days

I woke up around 7:00 AM and performed my normal routine of showering and getting dressed, this time reflecting on our last day at Hibiscus. Our last day in Ghana! We had done so much, it was hard to believe that we were about to go back to the U.S. Despite all the fun, we were all ready to return home.

Wakeelah stopped by my room and took my breakfast order. Today I was going to change my normal order and have French toast with fruit. We gathered in the lobby and went over to the dining room. The sun was hot, even early in the morning. Everyone seemed to be in a good mood.

Today, we were supposed to return to Auntie Josephine's bank and pick up the money that she was converting for us. We were running a little bit late, but we decided not to worry about it and relaxed.

Over our relatively leisurely breakfast, we started talking about NaNa Kow's predictions. Wakeelah asked me specifically how I felt about his comments regarding my estranged wife, specifically that I should be glad that she was not in my life. I told her that even though he said that and I sometimes felt that way, it was still very hard to deal with the emotional aspect of divorce. Wakeelah agreed, saying she could understand since she was going through some issues in her own marriage.

We finished eating then hooked up with Yao. Today he looked sharp. He had on a new shirt and new pants. We jumped in the truck and drove towards the bank. Auntie was looking sharp as usual and was ready with the money. She gave us excellent rates. When we tried to "dash" her for hooking us up, she would not have it, saying the idea was "cancelled!" We hugged her one more time and said goodbye. Man, I loved hugging her! She gave the best hugs!

On the way back, we stopped by the cultural center to pick up a few last minute gifts. Before going into the shopping area, I stopped to use the restroom. There was a brother sitting at a table outside the restroom where it seemed like he was reading the paper. I was stunned when he asked me to pay to use the facilities.

When I asked about this, one brother passed by me saying, "This is Africa, not America!" I told the guy I would pay on the way out. I went inside, and the restroom was about the foulest thing I had seen. I went into a stall to pay the water bill and prayed that nothing splashed on my feet since I had on open-toed Nike sandals. On the way out, I saw a brother paying the guy at the desk for the "privilege" of using the toilets. This time the brother at the desk tore off a sheet of newspaper and handed it to the guy. He wasn't reading, he was selling toilet paper! I said well I'll be damned...

I walked over to the cultural center to catch up with the crew. I searched out the brother whom I'd purchased from the day before. He was in his shop making bracelets. As I walked past the other vendors, they tried their best to persuade me to spend some money in their shop. They shouted things like, "You promised you would stop by my store!" when of course I hadn't. I guess they didn't take too kindly to me spending all my money with this one shop.

Lavelle and I bought our last gifts. While inside the shops, we ran into Lucy, the businesswoman with whom we had dinner. She was buying goods in bulk so she could ship them to the States to be sold at a higher price. Many of the shops in the U.S. that specialized in African goods received their merchandise in this manner. She had worked out a deal where she received a piece of the action. Smart lady.

A New Identity

I was glad to be done with all of my shopping. The ladies had a few more items to get. I was on total chill mode at that point. They ended up going into a jewelry shop. Yao and I sat outside and talked with one of the owners while they looked around. The shop owner introduced himself as "Elinya of the La people". I introduced myself as "James of the Krobos". That was the first time I had introduced myself that way, and it felt good. The guy approvingly shook his head and said "My mother's Krobo"[*].

Winding Down

After the ladies looked for a few more minutes, we finally left to go back to Hibiscus. Once we got there, we ran into Gifti and her son Kwasi. We presented them with their gifts, and they were extremely happy. We gave Kwasi a container to hold his sewing supplies and a small oil painting. We gave Gifti some Tupperware to store food. It's amazing how they cherished something that was seemingly so small to us. It really made me want to try harder to appreciate the smaller things in life.

After this nice moment, we went to our rooms to finish packing. We then went over to the guesthouse to settle our bills with August, My Man.

---

[*] It's customary for people to say their father's tribe as their tribe of origin. I used my mother's since that was all I knew.

We all sat with August one-on-one, and Monique was first. After she came out, you could tell that something wasn't right. Monique became upset at how August had treated her. August refused to accept her credit card, saying he needed cash to settle his payroll. This, along with the other service problems we encountered at Hibiscus, did not leave a good taste in our mouths. We finally got the bills straight and returned to the guesthouse.

Hibiscus was a nice place to lodge if you were in Accra, but they won't survive if they keep providing shoddy service. Wakeelah was going to have her work cut out for her if she ever returned to her training seminar.

After we returned to the guesthouse, I went to Lavelle's room and fell asleep for a while. Lavelle woke me up to help her find her camera. We eventually found it in one of her bags. After this exercise, we loaded Wakeelah's bags in the truck, then went back to the dining room for our last meal with Wakeelah before she went to the airport. Actually she was the only one eating. Since she was on standby, she had to get to the airport early.

After Wakeelah finished her meal, we left for the airport. As we were about to pull off, we heard a knock on the side of the truck. It was NaNa Kow, who had come to see Wakeelah off and give her some herbal medicines. I slid over and he rode in the front seat with me.

Yao drove us to the airport where we waited for Wakeelah's seat to be confirmed. While we waited, we laughed and reminisced about our trip. Wakeelah had taken to imitating the deep-voiced, attention grabbing brother from Labadi Beach. We all busted out laughing.

After about an hour wait, Wakeelah's seat was confirmed. We hugged her and watched as she ascended the steps to the boarding area. We wished our "mother" a safe journey. After all, she really watched over us during our trip, and we would never forget that.

We left the airport and found the truck. We got in and headed back towards Hibiscus. One of NaNa Kow's friends had joined us so we could give him a ride back to his house. Along the way, we also stopped to use the phone so we could call our relatives in the U.S. to confirm our flight information.

"Special Sauce"

As we pulled into the Hibiscus lot, my stomach was growling. I was ready to eat. We immediately went to the dining room. Na Na Kow stayed at the guesthouse, waiting for us to finish dinner. Tonight, Richard was cooking. He cooked well, but sometimes he seemed surly. Tonight was one of those times.

Richard cooked jollof rice, baked fish and vegetables, pretty much the usual. We all were wondering what was up because the portions of the fish were so small. When we asked Richard to cook some more, he said they didn't have any more fish, but that he would cook some chicken instead. We all joked that he would add some "special sauce" to the food since we were complaining.

He brought out the chicken and we threw down. I then asked him for some dessert. He tried to front and say they didn't have any. After asking him a series of questions, he finally admitted they had some fruit. He went back to the kitchen and reappeared a few minutes later with the fruit.

Our Final Evening at Hibiscus

While the ladies were talking, I began to watch the Euro Cup soccer semifinal on the TV. Several Hibiscus workers were also watching. It was a tightly contested match between Portugal and France. During the game, I received a call from NaNa Kow. He was wondering when we would return to the guesthouse so we could have our final rap session before we left.

I told him that we were on our way and that we would be there in a few minutes. I gathered everyone up so we could walk over. In a few minutes, we were at the guesthouse, where NaNa Kow was waiting for us in the lobby as he also watched the soccer game.

Everyone was already packed and we had given everyone their gifts. All we had to do now was relax and shoot the breeze until it was time to go. We ended up talking and watching the rest of the soccer game. France won to advance to the final in a pretty exciting game. We also made sure we had NaNa Kow's contact information so we could keep in touch.

As the game ended, it was finally time to leave for the airport. As we got in the truck, we needed to make room for a woman who needed a ride to the airport. She was in town for business and somehow got stranded without a ride to the airport, so the folks at Hibiscus decided to help her out.

After a 20-minute ride, we reached Kotoka International at 10:00 PM. Our flight didn't leave until midnight, so we had plenty of time. Since we had already checked our bags and confirmed our tickets, we all felt at ease.

'Til Next Time

We said our goodbyes to NaNa Kow and Yao and went inside the terminal. We eventually made our way to the first waiting area. There were several passengers already waiting. Many of them were American college

91

students returning to the U.S. Despite the late hour, they were full of that youthful energy that kept them talking endlessly.

After a brief stay in the waiting area, we all made our way to a long line where they X-rayed bags. The airport was humid, and this point was emphasized even more as we stood in line waiting for our bags to be X-rayed. As the line inched along this massive corridor, we passed a small AC wall unit that cooled an area of about three feet. Let's just say that somebody slightly underestimated the cooling power of that unit. We wanted to stay in front of the AC, but the line was slowly moving.

We finally got through the X-ray line and another ticket check before moving towards a second seating area. This area was much more crowded than the first one. The talkative students occupied the entire front section while families and business people took the remaining seats. Some people had the nerve to stretch out across three seats and go to sleep while others were forced to stand.

After what seemed like a long wait, the attendant finally announced the boarding arrangements. When the students' section was called, they stampeded through the corridor and descended down the steps. I couldn't help but think how funny it would have been if one of them fell. I know that's mean but they were kind of obnoxious. They finally called our section, and we followed the students' path.

We went down a flight of stairs where we waited for the shuttle to take us to the plane. The bus took us out to the tarmac and deposited us at the foot of the plane. We got off the bus and bum rushed an attendant who was supposedly checking tickets. We kind of just moved around him and then went up the steps to board the plane. All I can say is that you'd better not have any health problems trying to board one of these planes. You needed to be in some shape to haul your carry-ons up that long flight of stairs.

We made it up the steps and got settled into our seats. As our plane left African soil and flew into the indigo sky, I thought about all of the wonderful adventures that we'd just experienced. I was also glad that we had managed to get through the trip without making mortal enemies with one another. If anyone did have issues, they didn't show it.

Thursday, June 29, 2000

The Middle Passage

During our flight, Lavelle and I laughed hysterically at one of those blooper programs showing on the monitors while everyone else tried to sleep. I know the lady in front of me wasn't thrilled when I violently grabbed her headrest in a fit of laughter.

While we tripped, Lavelle's stomach was bothering her. It had been bothering her for several days, so she was being careful with what she ate on the flight. Surprisingly, Monique didn't have motion sickness.

The food was good, but I didn't eat too much since my body clock was all screwed up. After a small meal, I drifted off to sleep. I continued to go in and out of sleep for several hours. I finally woke up to see the faint rays of the early morning sun chasing us across the Atlantic. The sun finally peaked over the horizon at around 6:30 AM. I felt good because I knew that we'd be landing in New York shortly.

I looked out the window and saw ocean for as far as the eye could see. I was thinking about how uncomfortable it was to sit for nine hours in a cramped seat. This immediately triggered thoughts of what it must have been like to be packed in the belly of a ship for months, bobbing up and down on the choppy waters of the Atlantic with no knowledge of where you were going or when you would get there.

The worst we had to deal with was an occasional foul smelling restroom, but we could at least return to our seats. Our ancestors had no such luxuries. People were forced to defacate on themselves, vomit on themselves and then perhaps lie next to someone who had just died. All of this while lying shackled to hundreds of others in the hot confines of a ship's hull with no airflow. And here I was thinking about leg cramps. When I thought about our ancestors' experience, it definitely put any little bullshit discomfort I had into perspective. Man, those people were strong. I honestly didn't know if I could have survived such an ordeal.

Touchdown

Our plane touched down at JFK and everyone applauded. It seemed that everyone held their breath until they felt the familiar thud of the airplane's landing gear hitting the ground. Travelers always have that sliver of doubt

93

about the pilots' abilities until they proved that they could deliver the goods with a safe landing.

I could honestly say I was happy to be back in the States. We'd had a wonderful time, but as the saying goes, there's no place like home. We retrieved our bags and walked towards Customs. Since Lavelle and I were bringing back food for our mother, we had to have our packages inspected. The customs agents were inspecting a passenger's bag as we walked up. I didn't know what the lady ahead of us was transporting, but all I can say is that I saw things crawling in her bag. It was absolutely gross. The customs agent was so disgusted she turned away and waived Lavelle and I through the line. I was glad we didn't have to open our box, but I knew we wouldn't have anything like that to deal with.

We walked through the airport, feeling like world explorers returning home. Monique spotted her family in Arrivals Hall. They hugged us as we told them about our fantastic journey. We briefly thought about getting breakfast, but we all decided that the earlier we left, the earlier we would get home. So we passed on the meal. We hugged and kissed the Armstrong's goodbye, and headed for the bus that would take us to Port Authority.

I was surprised at how cool the weather was in New York for that time of year. I had on shorts and I was cold. On top of that, it started to rain. I was hoping that the bus would show up soon. We were supposed to meet Imakhus and give her some items from Ghana, so Lavelle called her to confirm our meeting. Imakhus informed Lavelle that she wouldn't be able to meet us and we could make other arrangements regarding the items. I was glad to hear this because I was ready to go home and didn't feel like making any more stops.

Grumpy Old Man

The Port Authority bus pulled up at about 10:30 AM. We put our bags on the bus and stepped on. A crotchety old bus driver who looked like he would give anything to be somewhere else ignored us. He made several pick-ups before we arrived at the Port Authority, glaring at people as they entered the bus.

He bobbed and weaved in and out of the heavy New York traffic, mumbling something under his breath. After dropping off several passengers at his first stop, he attempted to leave a man who was frantically trying to get his attention by running alongside of the moving bus. And you know the bus driver saw the man running in his side view mirror. The man had accidentally picked up the wrong bag. If it weren't for a station worker who had radioed the bus driver and asked him to stop, the driver would have left the man.

Lavelle's stomach was still bothering her, and since the bus driver was acting so funky, she decided to leave him a little something to remember her by in the bus restroom. The driver fought through the stop and go traffic and we finally arrived at the Port Authority.

The bus driver stood and watched as the passengers unloaded their own bags. I climbed into the hull of the bus to get the bags for one of the passengers, an older woman. She had on a dress and there was no way she would be able to get her bag without getting really dirty. The bus driver ignored all of us.

Once I got the bags, I went to get a baggage carrier to assist us. The guy who showed up was extremely helpful in getting us to our bus terminal. We arrived just in time to catch the very next bus out of New York going to D.C.

Ghana in D.C.

The bus ride was again uneventful, which was a good thing. We arrived at the Greyhound station in D.C. at 2:30 PM. Lavelle and I retrieved our luggage and looked for a cab to take us to Rocha's house. Seeing that "I need a cab" look on our faces, a driver approached us and asked if we needed a ride. We told him we did, and he replied, "Ah, I see you are coming from my country." He had noticed the Ghana Customs inspection stickers on our luggage.

As he put our bags in the cab's trunk, we started to tell him about our trip. As it turned out, he was from Kumasi, so of course we had to tell him about our near meeting with the Asantehene. He told us that his daughter was in Kumasi and that he was going back later on that year. He dropped us off at Rocha's house, where we picked up Lavelle's car. From there, we left for home.

The Future

We drove through the streets of D.C. and I was immediately struck by the similarities between people in D.C. and people in Ghana. The facial features. The walks. The body types. I couldn't help but think that here we were separated by an ocean but linked by our ancestors. I hope that more and more African-Americans will be able to make the trip that I was able to make. I plan on talking to everyone who'll listen about the trip and hope that my enthusiasm sparks an interest in them to want to see Africa for themselves.

At the very least, I hope that my ancestors are pleased that I was able to see where they walked and that I can now return home to tell part of their story. I look forward to returning to Africa to learn more about my people and myself so that in a small way I can help bridge the gap between Africa and America.

ABOUT THE AUTHOR

Mr. Gaines is a native of the Washington, D.C. area and a 1991 graduate of the University of Maryland. He is a first-time author who was so inspired by his first trip to Africa that he felt compelled to share his story. Mr. Gaines uses a warm and friendly writing style that makes the reader feel as though they are with him on his trip. His keen eye for details along with a witty sense of humor allows him to share his experiences in ways that connect with his audience. Mr. Gaines hopes to inspire others to visit their ancestral homelands so that they too can "shake hands" with their ancestors and gain a better understanding of who they are.

Printed in the United States
695700003B